VIRGINIA'S HAUNTED HISTORY

MICHELLE L. HAMILTON

Michelle L. Hamilton

First Edition:
First printing

Cover art by: Liliana Marie Creative

Michelle L. Hamilton

PUBLISHED BY HAUNTED ROAD MEDIA, LLC
www.hauntedroadmedia.com

United States of America

To Mom and Dad
with much love.

Michelle L. Hamilton

Acknowledgments

Thank you, dear reader, for picking up this book. Currently in the paranormal field there are many fantastic authors producing wonderful books that you, the reader, can select. The fact that you have decided to spend your hard-earned money to purchase this book and spend a few hours reading my work means a lot to me.

I would like to thank the following people:

To Mom and Dad, thank you for all the love and support you have both given me.

To my poodles Belle and Violet for being the best "research and writing assistants" and for reminding me when to get away from the computer to take them for a walk.

To Mike Ricksecker and Haunted Road Media for giving me a platform to publish my books.

A huge thanks to Amanda R. Woomer and Troy Taylor for publishing my articles in *The Feminine Macabre* and *The Morbid Curious*.

I wish to also to thank my amazing staff at the Mary Washington House for putting up with me when I talk about ghosts and the paranormal.

To Alex Matsuo for your friendship and support during a difficult time. Thank you for letting me join the Association of Paranormal Study. I look forward to working with Alex, Jason Scott Roach, and Ted Willis.

Michelle L. Hamilton

Table of Contents

Michelle L. Hamilton

Introduction

Each of my books started with a question, in this case I wanted to know if people encountered ghosts in Virginia during the 19th-century. As you can see from the following pages, the answer is yes—people in Virginia had encounters with the paranormal before and after the Civil War. In my previous book *Haunted Land: Ghosts, Witches, and Divination in the 18th-Century*, I uncovered a murder case in 1737, where the perpetrator confessed after he believed the victim's ghost was haunting him.

While people were seeing ghosts, it only became wildly reported in newspapers and journals in the 1850s. The main reason behind the sudden interest of with ghosts in the 1850s was the birth of Spiritualism in 1848. Spiritualism was belief that it was possible for the living to speak with the dead. Ghost stories, both real and fictional, were published to whet the appetite of the public.

As you will see, the press' treatment of the paranormal has not changed, as the accounts of the paranormal are generally treated as a comical novelty. Used to reinforce the journalists prejudices against women and minorities. But for those who encountered the paranormal, it was a serious and frequently terrifying experience. For the people featured in these accounts to come forward took tremendous bravery as they faced the possibility of being ridiculed and ostracized by their community.

The trauma of the Civil War left literally and physically scars upon the land of Virginia and on its residents. While the reports of ghost sightings were limited during the war that changed after the war. During Reconstruction and the Gilded Age, newspapers in the state were full of reports of ghosts and paranormal activity, many tied to sites connected to the Civil War.

For me the Reconstruction era is one of the most painful and disappointing periods in American history. The period started with the promise of equality for African Americans as the nation strove to rectify the sins of the past. Sadly, it proved to be a mirage, and the Gilded Age witnessed the stripping of equal rights for African Americans. The ghosts witnessed during Reconstruction and the Gilded Age reflected the political and societal tumult of the era. Unhappy wraiths stalked the streets of Virginia's cities and communities.

Ghosts were used to settle personal grievances and to reinforce racial divides. This aspect of the paranormal has largely been forgotten by researchers and historians of the supernatural. Many of the stories and accounts are reproduced here for the first time since there original publication. Sadly, many of the locations featured in this book have been lost to history. Where possible, I have located images of the sites featured.

The reader will find the language of the some of the accounts featured to be appalling. As I have already mentioned, journalists of the 19th-century used the reports of paranormal activity to reinforce their racist views of African Americans and other minority groups. I have included the accounts to present an honest picture of life in 19th-century Virginia. Sadly, the reports and witness testimony of people of color have been overlooked in the history of the paranormal. I wanted to give those who have previously been neglected their chance to share their stories with the respect and dignity that were denied them at the time of the original publication. I also wanted to show the horrendous treatment they received from the press.

Virginia's Haunted History

The stories reproduced here have a little bit for everybody. You will found accounts that I personally found to be among some of the creepiest paranormal accounts that I have ever come across. Others are of a more humorous nature (or more accurately examples of 19th-century humor). There are also examples of hoaxes, committed either for profit or for the persecution of African Americans.

These stories are reported verbatim as they appeared at the time of publication. I have some edits for clarity and a few corrections in spelling and punctuation. I hope you find the following accounts as fascinating and as illuminating as I have.

Part I

Antebellum
1850 - 1859

The Richmond Dispatch, Richmond, Virginia, March 19, 1852, pg. 2.

A RACE NOT BEFORE REPORTED.

Once upon a time, as the traditions generally begin—but it was not a very long time ago—there lived a ferryman at one of the ferries upon the Staunton river. This ferryman was a good, weak-minded, tall and muscular man; but he was not distinguished for courage. He was remarkable for his superstitious belief in ghosts and spirits. But "inspiring, bold John Barleycorn"[1] could never dispel the fears of ghosts which nightly haunted the mind of our ferryman. He treasured vividly in his recollection all the strange events, the murders, suicides, violent deaths of that region, which had happened in his day, and a number which were the traditions of days before his time. So that there was scarcely a turn in a neighboring road, or a neighboring farm, that was, in the belief of the ferryman, without its spirits revisiting the "glimpses of the moon" in their disquietude

---

[1] Alcohol

at the unsatisfactory terminations of their earthly existence.—Loth was this ferryman to turn out from his bed to obey the loud call of the traveller on the opposite side of the river, who, at dead of night, wanted to be put over. On a cloudy night it was more than he dare do to go out amongst the spirits of the drowned that nightly hovered about the stream. On such a night the belated traveller had to give over the prosecution of his journey, and turn back to hunt for a place to rest; for our ferryman made it a point never to hear him.

In the neighborhood there lived a planter—a fine portly gentleman, somewhat beyond the middle age of life—a jovial old gentleman—a sample of Virginia planters of the time—surrounded by plenty—fond of a good joke—at peace with "all the world and the rest of mankind"—and if he seldom said his prayers, his animosities were neither many nor bitter, and no man ever turned away from his door hungry and fatigued. Our planter was fond of a joke, as we have said—nay, he was a practical joker, and would take great pains to plain and carry out his conceits in this way.

The planter had a sort of kind regard for the ferryman, whose singularities very much amused him, and the ferryman never went reluctantly to the planter's house, for, besides the general kind treatment he met, he was always sure to find some very good brandy there…By the side of the path-way leading from the ferry to the planter's house, there was a grave yard! The ferryman had never been known to pass this after dark.

One afternoon the ferryman called to see the planter, and while there, the time passed most agreeably—the ferryman told some of his most startling ghost stories, and the planter, in return some of his anecdotes, which the ferryman relished the better, as he took them along with the brandy. As the sun began to decline in the West, the ferryman became uneasy, and wanted to be off to reach home before dark. His host, professing to be greatly pleased with his agreeable company, begged him to stay to supper, and promised to send a negro man with him to keep him company home. A good supper, with this promise of an escort, was more than the ferryman could resist, so he staid [stayed].

It was near on to twelve when the ferryman and his companion left the hospitable mansion of the planter. Side by side walked the two, and as they neared the grave-yard, the ferryman placed his sable escort between him and that dreaded habitations of the dead. He resolved not to look that way; but involuntarily his eyes stole a glance—when, horrible to relate!—he beheld a slow-moving white figure, rising from amidst the graves! For an instant he was fixed with terror; but the figure made a step forward—his muscles immediately yielded to the impulse of his affrightened brain—and he bounded off in the direction of his home with all his might. He had not gone far before he heard rapidly falling feet shortening the distance between him and them. He mended his pace, and was afraid for a time to look behind to see whether it was his escort or the ghost; at last he snatched a glimpse over his shoulder and beheld the white figure in close pursuit! And now the race grew in interest. The ferryman strained every sinew—he neither turned to the right nor to the left, but leaped over stumps and stones, and dashed through mud-holes. The white figure followed in the same style. If the steps of the ferryman flagged, the gaining sounds of the fast-following feet lent him fresh vigor, while the increasing speed of the ferryman seemed to impart additional facility to the nimble locomotion of his mysterious pursuer.

Through the tall, dense forest of the river hills ran the narrow path of the ferry. Animals, terrestrial and amphibious, usual to such a locality, filled the air with nocturnal noises, which paused at different points in the route as the swift moving figures fled by. The great horned-owl hooted—the screech owl screeched—the frogs from their bogs and streams among the ravines, lifted up their voices in deafening and dismal chorus—and the flickering lights of the fire-fly lamp glimmered among the trees. Appalling to mortals, delightful to demons, were the sounds that rang and reverberated through the forest. The quiet solo of the katy-did was the only friendly voice that saluted the air. But more terrible than all else to the ferryman was the mysterious spirit that pursued him with a speed that his almost superhuman effort could not surpass. At any other time, at that place, and that hour, each several sound would have made the ferryman's heart sink within him; he would have seen a devil in every bush; but now every source of apprehension and terror was shut up and overwhelmed by the great and impending danger which hung upon his rear.

On swept our fleet and rapid runners. Terror lent the ferryman his wings, and some mysterious impulse hurried on the white figure; which, in spite of all his efforts, gained a little on the ferryman. Up and down hill—over ditch and stream—there was no pause in their flight, and in their last down hill sweep, before the goal was reached, they seemed to skim over the ground without the aid of feet. All things have an end, and so had this race. At last the goal—the ferryman's house—was won. A long way from that domicile, on the river bank, however, the feet of the runners were heard—great was the astonishment of the family at the ferry, and they listened in breathless anxiety as the feet came nearer, and they heard the hard breathing of the competitors; but the greater still was their amazement when the ferryman fell exhausted at the door, and soon after fell at his side the white figure!—Lights were brought, and immediate assistance was given to the poor ferryman who was more dead than alive. The white figure terrified them all; but was finally cautiously approached and unwrapped and was found to be one of the planter's negro men!

When the boy, who went to escort the ferryman returned and told how the race began, his master laughed so loud and free that he is said to have awakened some of his neighbors a mile off! "But the rascal in the sheet," said he, "why did he follow the ferryman so far?—That was more than he was told to do. But he has made the joke all the better, a rascal! He shall have an extra drink for it;" and

18

the planter shook his sides again.

The next day it was found that the negro in the sheet was much terrified as the ferryman. As he rose, a briar had caught the sheet, and supposing the devil to be after him for endeavoring to scare the ferryman, he ran for life and death! When this appendix to the story was made known to the planter he went off into a fit of laughter that endured so long as to alarm his friends.

And this is a race never before written down—a race that the performances of Gildersleeve, and the American deer cannot be compared with—a race, which, for the speed and bottom of the runners, might rank with the achievements of the Eclipses, the Henrys of the turf, and the Boston of later years—Boston! whose death our neighbor, of the Whig, considered a public calamity. Carrier pigeons and the winds of a white squall, could be scarcely considered more fleet. Grass never was known to grow in the runners' tracks!

This remarkable race, was long the talk of the neighborhood, and afforded our venerable friend the planter, many a hearty laugh in the evening of his days. He considered it the best of his practical jokes. The ferryman soon recovered from the effects of his fright; he heartily forgave the trick, and was treated with additional kindness at the planter's; but he never again took supper from home!

The Richmond Dispatch, Richmond, Virginia, September 29, 1852, pg. 1.

THE HAUNTED HOUSE.—On the Southern back of the river, about a mile west of this city, stands upon a very conspicuous eminence a large old brick house, familiar to the eyes of all citizens of Richmond, and known as "the haunted house." There it has stood, for nearly fifty years, "solitary and alone," the cold winds whistling through its open windows, a monument of all that is dreary and desolate. How it obtained the cognomen of "the haunted house," we know not. Feeling a desire to know something of the history of this celebrated abode of ghosts and hobgoblins, we were induced, a few days ago, to pay it a visit. We found none of the frightful family at home. Rawhead and bloody bones[2] were not there. For half an hour we sojourned within its barren and silent walls, the only ghost to be seen or heard. Nor could we discover any signs of ghosts from

THE DAILY DISPATCH

JAS. A. COWARDIN, Proprietor.
HUGH R. PLEASANTS, Editor.

THE HAUNTED HOUSE.—On the Southern bank of the river, about a mile west of this city, stands upon a very conspicuous eminence a large old brick house, familiar to the eyes of all the citizens of Richmond, and known as "the haunted house." There it has stood, for nearly fifty years, "solitary and alone," the cold winds whistling through its open windows, a monument of all that is dreary and desolate. How it obtained the cognomen of "the haunted house," we know not. Feeling a desire to know something of the history of this celebrated abode of ghosts and hobgoblins, we were induced, a few days ago, to pay it a visit. We found none of the frightful family at home. Rawhead and bloody bones were not there. For half an hour we sojourned within its barren and silent walls, the only ghost to be seen or heard. Nor could we dis-

another world having been there; although there were abundant evidences of a large number of the spirits of this world having paid a visit. The hand-writings upon the wall, and other signs, showed that the most mischievous ghosts of all, the living spirits of this world, had haunted it more than the dead ghosts of another world. There were no spirits there, "black or white," living or dead, to hold converse with us, either in relation to the history of the house, the affairs of this, or of the things of the world to come. But, our visit was not an unprofitable one. We came away pleased that we had made it; for we obtained one of the most pleasing, beautiful, and magnificent views of Richmond and all the surrounding country, that we ever beheld. We found that that old house occupies the highest point and commands the most extensive and charming view of any location in all this region. A more delightful place for a residence is nowhere to be found in this vicinity of Richmond. From no other point can be obtained so full, accurate, and beautiful view

---

[2] Names for an English bogeyman used to scare children. Bloody Bones, also called Rawhead, was a water demon believed to haunt deep ponds, oceans, and marl pits where it drowned children.

of Richmond, the river scenery, and all the surrounding country. It commands a fine view at every point of the compass, embracing Manchester, Rocketts, Richmond, the River, Islands and Bridges, the Canal, &c. Here is a choice spot for the exercise of the artist's pencil, or the painter's brush. At 5 o'clock in the evening, (the hour at which we visited "the haunted house,") when the declining sun is gilding the houses, steeples, bridges, &c., with a silvery brightness, a scene of almost unequalled beauty is presented. A view such as would have compensated us for a walk of at least ten instead of two miles. We are surprised that no one ever thought of making that his local habitation—The walls of the house are still apparently as good as ever, (to the credit of the bricklayer be it said) and the slate-roof, but little worse for wear. The interior of the house, although originally finished (as far as completed) in the best style, has received much damage from the mischievous ghosts who have haunted the house from Richmond and elsewhere, and needs repairs. There is a fine spring of water on the river bank, just below the house, and everything inviting except alone the ghosts. But, we apprehend, they would be the least troublesome of all spirits.

Richmond, from the hill above the waterworks ca. 1830.
Engraving by W.J. Bennett from a painting by G. Cooke; Published by Lewis P. Clover, New York. (Image courtesy of Wikipedia).

The "Haunted House," we understand, was built near fifty years ago, by two gentlemen of the names of Winston and Waddell, who purchased the land adjacent to the river there for the purpose of erecting a milling establishment. After they had proceeded so far as the erection of a dam across the stream to Belle Isle, had laid the foundation of their mills and had erected the house of which we have been speaking, on the hill immediately above their mill seat, it was discovered that their dam backed the water upon the cotton factory mills of their neighbors immediately above. An injunction and suit at law put a stop to further operations, and finally, after incurring considerable labor and expense, the mill, dwelling house, &c., were all abandoned and unimproved ever since. But, the day is not distant, we predict, when this property will claim a much higher estimate than at present, and when a great change will come over the face of things round and about "the haunted house."

The Richmond Dispatch, Richmond, Virginia, August 3, 1853, pg. 1.

The Examiner also has an elaborate and very interesting article on "Ghost Mania," referring to many remarkable delusions in past days and their solutions. It contends that after the exposure of all unnatural and mysterious performances—that after the proof, "that whatever conflicts with the revelations of the Bible and the experience of mankind for three thousand years, is the result of imposture, of jugglery, of sleight of hand and knavish trickery,"—"it is disgraceful that the people of the United States should be made the laughing stock of the civilized world, by the numberless humbugs that afflict the land!" This is too true.

The American Union, Morgantown, Virginia [West Virginia], November 12, 1853, pg. 2.

From the Wheeling Gazette.
SINGULAR ARRAIR.

We have a relation from a gentleman of Wetzel county of a singular character, and give it for what it is worth. It is at least sufficient to show this fact, that with all the intelligence of the present age, there is no doubt that the impression of physical communication with the spirit world, which was antecedent to Plato, and coeval[3] with scripture history, is not yet eradicated from all minds.

The affair to which we refer is related to us by a man of fair intelligence and honest *belief*.

Some three years ago, as his story goes, two men named Gamble and Mercer, residing near or on Peyton's Island, started to cross the Ohio river in a skiff, loaded with barrels, about sunset.

They were a little tight,[4] as well as the barrels. One barrel fell overboard, and for fear of upsetting the skiff they dragged the barrel to the shore, from whence they started, and Mercer thinking of some business about a mile below, as he reported, went down to attend to it, leaving Gamble with the skiff. A little boat coming up about the time, found a skiff capsized and the barrels floating. Mercer only said that he had left Gamble. Some suspicions attached to Mercer, but he was never apprehended.

These suspicions grew out of the fact that he had borrowed money of Gamble and had given him a note against a man as security. During the afternoon previous he had asked Gamble to give him the note, but he was refused. A few weeks after the note was presented to the drawer and paid, for the benefit of Mercer.

---

[3] To have the same date of origin.
[4] Drunk

Some four months after a body was found in the river, supposed to have been Gamble's, and the whole matter died away, until some weeks since, when as the story goes, as some gentlemen from in and around New Martinsville, with whom was Mr. Hindman, a very respectable tavernkeeper there, had been across the river, to a husking party. Returning home, they agreed before getting to the river, to have a race, the one getting there last to pay all the ferriage. Mr. H. cut across a field, and in passing through it he met a hatless man who told him that he was Gamble,—had been murdered by Mercer for this note, that his body was buried in such a place, that he must have Mercer apprehended, and he would confess sufficient circumstances to have him held over to a circuit court term, when he would be convicted of murder. Hindman had never seen Gamble; but, it is said, he described him accurately. Mercer was apprehended, circumstances soon transpired that it is thought would serve to convict Mercer, who was to be tried before a called court, on Saturday last, at New Martinsville. We shall probably hear the result one of these days. In the meantime we say nothing more to the [unclear] we have heard and we do not suppose that it is true; and further that we cannot believe in the statement unless we can be privileged to have ocular demonstration, though it is reported that it has had a bad effect on friend Hindman—that he looks as though he had "a long sick," and could not get over it.

The American Union, Morgantown, Virginia [West Virginia], November 19, 1853, pg. 2.

THE GHOST.

Mr. WOLF sends a long account of the affair at New Martinsville relative to the murder of Gamble and the apprehension of Mercer for the murder. It is entirely the same as the one we published from the mouth of a citizen of New Martinsville, some few days since. We omit, therefore, all of his communication that corresponds with our report, and publish the later particulars ascertained by Mr. Wolf. He speaks of Hindman's interview with the spirit and says:

From the Times & Gazette.
NEW MARTINSVILLE, Wetzel Co., Va.
Saturday, Oct. 29, 1853.

When Mr. Hindman came up with his company, they were wondering at his delay. He immediately charged them with practicing a deception on him, and stated what had occurred; with one accord they declared their innocence. This deepened the impression on the mind of Hindman. He could not sleep during that night, he returned to the same place, about the same hour of the night, in order to satisfy himself whether any person could have escaped without detection. Having done this, according to direction, he sent for Mercer and propounded to him certain questions which had been arranged by his nocturnal visitor. Mercer came; and his conduct was such as to excite still stronger suspicions and on the affidavit of Mr. H. he was arrested and on this day underwent an examination.

It appeared on the examination, that on the night of the murder, Mercer came home wet all over; that he gave a false account of how he got wet. On the next evening he exhibited one of the witnesses the note of Wightman which Gamble had refused to let him have, stating to witness that there was a balance of seven dollars yet due, which would have been paid, but Gamble had nothing less than $10; but another witness testified that Gamble had five dollar bills. He also gave contradictory accounts of the last time he saw Gamble. This excited suspicion in the mind of Mr. Wait who was stopping for the night, and he could not sleep. During the night Mercer seemed uneasy and restless. At one time he said, "Gamble I must have it;" then jumped out on the floor saying, "Gamble, I'll be damned if I don't have it." By this time he awakened, and after ascertaining, as he thought, that all were asleep he went to bed; frequently during the night he would grapple violently with his brother, who with difficulty could release himself.

The note he collected, and three dollars from the widow, making $11 more than his claim.—Shortly after Gamble's decease, several large claims in the hands of the Sheriff against Mercer were paid, and property bought, and no one knew where the money came from. Mr. Wait was warned at the peril of his life, not to repeat what he heard and saw, and other suspicious conduct was proven against him. After his arrest he tried to get a witness to swear falsely—to feign sickness, or to run off. The witness through fear, feigned sickness, but the doctor settled that point, and he was brought forward, and under oath declared as above.

The boat, stocking, and a piece of the pants were brought from the grave and identified.—The cloth answered precisely to Mr. Hindman's description.

Mr. H. delivered his whole narrative under oath, not as matter of evidence, but simply to show cause why he had been induced to have Mercer arrested.

After the examination Mercer was remanded to jail for a further

THE GHOST.

Mr. Wolf sends a long account of the affair at New Martinsville relative to the murder of Gamble and the apprehension of Mercer for the murder. It is entirely the same as the one we published from the mouth of a citizen of New Martinsville, some few days since. We omit, therefore, all of his communication that corresponds with our report, and publish the later particulars ascertained by Mr. Wolf. He speaks of Hindman's interview with the spirit and says:

From the Times & Gazette.

NEW MARTINSVILLE, Wetzel Co., Va.
Saturday, Oct. 29, 1853.

When Mr. Hindman came up with his company, they were wondering at his delay. He immediately charged them with practicing a deception on him, and stated what had occurred; with one accord they declared their innocence. This deepened the impression on the mind of Hindman. He could not sleep hearing.

Taking it altogether there is a strong array of circumstantial testimony fixing clearly in the public mind the guilt of the prisoner. But it remains to be seen, what a jury will do in the case.

This you will perceive is making a practical matter out of spiritual manifestations. And in the minds of reasonable men must amount to an actual demonstration. A few more cases of this kind will prove a terror alike to evil doers and unbelieving bigots, who think there is nothing in Heaven or earth, not found in their theology.

By the time this nut is fairly cracked, perhaps there will be another. I commend it to the consideration of all reasonable men. J.B. WOLF.

N. B.—You will find every item in this statement essentially true. As I gathered them from the witnesses, prosecuting attorney and other responsible men.

The Richmond Dispatch, Richmond, Virginia, November 23, 1853, pg. 4.

THE WETZEL COUNTY GHOST.—The Fairmont Republican gives, through a correspondent, the result of the examination of Laban Mercer, charged with the murder of Gamble. This extraordinary case excites great interest.

Mercer was tried before the County Court, and after a protracted investigation into the matter, was sent on for further trial to the Circuit Court, that is to say, at the next spring term of the Court. The correspondent goes on to say:

Every man, woman, and child in this county, (with a few exceptions,) believe in his guilt, and would hang him right away if permitted by the authorities. For my own part, I don't honestly believe that there is sufficient evidence to convict Mercer or any one for the supposed murder; and I think it will appear that so far from

Gamble's being murdered, the probability is that he was drowned. To be sure, there are some slight grounds for suspicion, but no more. A Wetzel County Jury, however, would now say "Guilty," beyond any doubt whatever.

The Cooper's Clarksburg Register, Clarksburg, Virginia [West Virginia], November 30, 1863, pg. 2.

A Ghost Story.

The citizens of Wetzel, and the adjoining counties, have been no little excited during the past few weeks by the appearance of a dead man, in his own proper person, among them. According to the popular supposition, this ghost bodes harm to some body, and it seems that one man is likely to have his neck put in jeopardy upon the strength of his visit. But we let a correspondent from "the sod," to the Wheeling Argus, tell the tale, as one most likely to get it correct.

The Cooper's Clarksburg Register, Clarksburg, Virginia [West Virginia], November 30, 1853, pg. 2.

N. MARTINSVILLE, Nov. 4.

MR. EDITOR:—I see in your last week's issue an article in reference to the apprehension of a man in this county for the high crime of murder, and the ground of the accusation rests upon a revelation from the other world, and that the whole evidence of the guilt of the party charged was communicated to a certain individual by a ghost, and upon the ghost's representation a man was deprived of his liberty and incarcerated in a prison. Now, sir, my object in writing this communication is to disabuse the public mind in reference to the whole matter, and to vindicate our courts from the imputation of acting upon evidence derived from ghosts. In the first place, it is a case that has produced a wonderful excitement in this and the surrounding communities. But, sir, to the facts of the case. Three years ago the 12th of this month, one John Gamble was in this place, and in the evening he left to go home, some four miles, in a skiff. When he left he had between two and three hundred dollars in money with him. About two miles below town some raftsmen that were lying at the shore, caught the skiff and some barrels that were in it when he started.

Gamble was found afterwards down near Ray's run, and he had no money or papers or any thing else on his person when found, and his pocket in his pantaloons was cut off. Many circumstances went to point out Leban Mercer as the guilty person, and public opinion had settled down upon the fact that Mercer was guilty, if the evidence could be got at. Things rested so until two weeks ago, when a party left town to go to a neighboring town to a corn-husking, and on their return home two o'clock at night, it being a remarkably clear night, and the moon was full, so that it was as light as moonlight could be, Mr. John H. Hindman, the worthy proprietor of the Wetzel House, in this place, took across Robert W. Cox's farm, whilst the company went around the road, and out in the middle of one of Cox's fields he states under oath that a person all at once appeared to him, and when he first saw whatever it was, it was a little to the left hand and about three feet from him, and the person or ghost was in the act of speaking, and he stated that the first words spoken were these: "You don't know me," and Hindman answered that he did not. Then the person, or ghost, or whatever you may call it, said "I am John Gamble, the man that was murdered by Leban Mercer. Your courts have not done me justice. I want you to have him arrested, and they will do me justice."

And after some other conversation the person or apparition

disappeared all at once from his view in the midst of a large level field on the river bottom, and what is very remarkable about the case, Hindman is, like myself, a great disbeliever in ghosts and hobgoblins, and perhaps if I had told the story the people would have ridiculed the matter, but Hindman is a man of such strict truth and veracity, and above all, so cool and self-possessed under all circumstances, and free and from excitement, that all who knew him did not for a moment doubt what he stated was true, and especially the next morning after, (although he had never seen Gamble and was not acquainted with him,) he described his size, appearance and clothing exactly as they were when Gamble left town. Friend Cox saw Gamble on the evening of his death, and he says that the description that Hindman gave of him (without knowing anything about how Gamble was dressed, his size, &c.,) was correct. Then after all this, Hindman had an interview with Mercer, and from certain statements and confessions made by Mercer to him, which in his mind convinced him of Mercer's guilt, and accordingly he swore out a warrant and was apprehended, but not upon the evidence drawn from the ghost, he was brought up for trial and it was found that Gamble loaded his skiff below town, alongside of R. W. Cox's farm, that he went out to the hill, where a man by the name of Whiteman lives, that Mercer came along, that they started to the river to Gamble's skiff, that after dark, two boys coming up the river saw them, and Gamble had a great deal of money, and was a little intoxicated; that he started down the bank to go home, that after his death, Mercer had a note of fifty-three dollars given by M. & J. Whiteman to Gamble, which Gamble had in his possession when he left Whiteman's to go to the river with Mercer, about dark, and that Mercer went home that night wet and muddy, although it was a dry night; and the fact of his having money afterwards, and various contradictory statements made by Mercer about where he saw Gamble last, and many other circumstances pointing to Mercer as the guilty person, and the court sent him on for further trial. Now you have the ghost story and the consequences attending it. Hindman does not say it was a ghost, but that it was something mysterious to him.

Yours &c.
WETZEL.

The *Richmond Enquirer*, Richmond, Virginia, December 2, 1853, pg. 1.

Laban Mercer, who was arrested for murder in Wetzel county, Virginia, on the accusation of the alleged ghost of John Gamble, as narrated in our last, has actually had his preliminary examination and has been ordered for further trial.

The *Richmond Dispatch*, Richmond, Virginia, December 23, 1853, pg.

A GHOST.—On Friday of last week a negro was hung near this place and buried. On Saturday night two or three young disciples of Aesculapius,[5] "intent upon prosecuting the science," determined to exhume the "subject" for the purpose of dissection. These, with a few supernumeraries, together with two or three negroes to perform the labor, repaired to the graveyard of the colored people, when they were taken all aback by an unearthly sound! The negroes were at work in the grave, the youngsters all standing around in silence,

---

[5] Roman god of medicine.

when hark! upon the midnight air a deep and thrilling groan is heard! The night was calm and still, not a leaf moved upon its stem, and millions of dew-drops lay sparkling in the moonlight like spangles upon an ancient costume! It was just such a night as a ghost would pick to walk abroad in! All in breathless silence, with "hair on end," looking in the direction whence the sound proceeded, when, sudden as thought, a tall and ghastly looking form stood before them, clad in the habiliments of the tomb! A wild and terrific scream escaped the lips of some of the company, who fled in dismay in various directions, whilst others, it is said, frightened out of the use of their limbs, stood rooted to the spot! The negroes, with a yell, bounded from the half-opened grave and fled, one of them declaring that the *day* of judgment had come in the *night*, and that he saw at least a hundred spectres bursting from the graves! One or two of the followers of Galen,[6] it is said, took the road to Tennessee, and might have been running yet, had not their legs refused to perform their office. The ghost was a mischievous wag who, thirsting to see a foot-race, enveloped his person in a sheet and concealed himself in the grave yard. He not only saw a foot-race, but had the pleasure, before the fun was over, of an *experimental knowledge* of how fast a ghost has to run to keep from being pelted to death with brick-bats!—*Abington Virginian.*

The Wheeling Daily Intelligencer, Wheeling, Virginia [West Virginia], April 18, 1854, pg. 3.

THE TRIAL of the man in Wetzel county, for murder connected with the famous "Ghost story," comes off this week. Hon. S. Clemens, of this city is one of the counsel for the prisoner.

---

[6] Galen (129 CE-c. 210 CE) was a Greek physician, surgeon, and philosopher who lived in Rome.

The Wheeling Daily Intelligencer, Wheeling, Virginia [West Virginia], April 24, 1854, pg. 3.

WETZEL CIRCUIT COURT.—THE GHOST STORY.—The trial of Laban Mercer for the murder of John Gamble, involving the alleged and mysterious appearance of the murdered man or his ghost, or something that looked like him, four years after his death, and upon which alleged circumstance Mercer was arrested—commenced in Wetzel county on Wednesday last. The testimony on both sides having been closed, we learn that the argument for the prosecution was commenced on Thursday by W. H. OLDHAM, Esq., of Marshall county, and that S. Clemens, A. T. Haywood, Cock and Horner, Esqrs., followed for the defense. We are not further advised in regard to the case.

The Richmond Enquirer, Richmond, Virginia, April 28, 1854, pg. 2.

GHOSTLY EVIDENCE.—A trial for murder took place last week, in Wetzel county, Va., in which the evidence rested mainly upon spirit rapping and ghost-seeing proof. A man named Laban Mercer was charged with the murder of a man named Gamble, some time since. A John Hindman met one night the ghost of the murdered man, who stated that Mercer was his murderer; and the spirit rappers were consulted, and they corroborated the evidence of the ghost. The Court, however, ruled out all such testimony, and Laban was acquitted. The trial created great interest in the part of the State where it occurred. Incredulous Court! not to believe, when the dead rise up to testify!

Michelle L. Hamilton

The Wheeling Daily Intelligencer, Wheeling, Virginia [West Virginia], May 5, 1854, pg. 3.

TESTIMONY OF A GHOST.—A trial is now going on in Wetzel county, Va., for a murder committed in 1850. The evidence is based upon the testimony of a man who met a ghost in the woods several times, which informed him that "Mr. Mercer" was the murderer. We had no idea that the *spirit-rapping humbug* had extended to the backwoods of western Virginia.—*Wash. Sentinel.*

The ghost aforesaid, like spirits called from the vasty deep, and who *don't* come, did not make his appearance at the trial, and his testimony as delivered to the man in the woods was not admitted, and the accused was acquitted. The ghost is held responsible for a contempt of court.

The American Union, Morgantown, Virginia [West Virginia], May 6, 1854, pg. 3.

Charged with Murder by a Ghost.

Laban Mercer was put on trial in Wetzel county, Va, on Wednesday last charged with the murder of John Gamble. The murder was committed in 1850, and subsequently the body of the deceased was found floating in the Ohio river, but no clue was had to the author of the deed until last fall, when a respectable citizen of the county went before a magistrate and made affidavit that a ghost had confronted him after night, in the woods, and told him that Mercer was the murderer of Gamble. The jury acquitted Mercer of the murder, for the want of sufficient testimony. The testimony of Mr. John Hindman that he saw the ghost of Gamble, was ruled out as was also the testimony of a man who slept in Mercer's room, and heard him in his sleep cry out to Gamble that he would have the money. The circumstantial evidence against Mercer was very strong, but in the opinion of the jury not sufficient to convict him.

The Wheeling Daily Intelligencer, Wheeling, Virginia [West Virginia], November 12, 1857, pg. 3.

That Ghost!—We gave a short time since, an account of the performances of a certain ghost which held its frightful vigils near a ravine not far from this city. As we anticipated that ghost has turned out to be a humbug—a self made ghost. Some of the young men caught him the other evening as he was "walking the night," moaning like a town bull with the mulligrubs,[7] and pommeled him until he yelped for quarter. The bogus ghost lives in the neighborhood, and had entered into an engagement to represent Hamlet's father for ten consecutive nights, and in consideration therefore was to receive five dollars from a young man who wanted to frighten his sweetheart (we guess they call them so) and, induce her, by ghostly advice to marry him. We publish this finale of the ghost story because we deem it sufficiently delightful for the present

---

[7] To be in an despondent, sullen, or ill-tempered mood.

incredulous state of the public mind. Our readers should receive it as they do eastern small bills.

The Wheeling Daily Intelligencer, Wheeling, Virginia [West Virginia], June 19, 1858, pg. 3.

A *Somnambulist.*—Yesterday morning about one o'clock, an acquaintance of ours, in going home from a roystering symposium, met on Market street, what he supposed to be a ghost in the sickly moonlight, but what afterwards turned out to be a well known citizen, in model artist costume, sans pantaloons, sans coat, sans everything but a shirt. The prevailing wind was making gentle dalliance with the extremity of his only garment; his eyes were fixed and staring wildly, and our informant having no idea that the monstrosity belonged to this earth, took a circuit about twenty yards around and hurried on. Our informant seeing the object "fetch up," and at the same time meeting a companion, took courage and proposed to go and see what it was and what it meant. Accordingly they approached and recognized a well known citizen, who, it appears, is a somnambulist, and who was out enjoying a soporific promenade. He was soon aroused to consciousness, and immediately afterwards struck a three minute gait for home, his sails swelling out in the most extensive and fashionable style.

Part II

The Civil War
1860 - 1865

The Wheeling Daily Intelligencer, Wheeling, Virginia [West Virginia], May 28, 1860, pg. 3.

OPTICAL illusions have often led to a belief in ghosts or spirits. In conversing with a friend recently, says an exchange, who is a most decided unbeliever in the supernatural, he mentioned a fact of his own experience. Awakening one night from sleep, he saw distinctly before him, looking through the thick wall of darkness, an eye intensely bright, large, luminous, and with an expression of terrible malignity. He rose up in his bed, and being a man of firm nerves, looked calmly at the singular apparition. It seemed slowly to approach him, until it rested just as the foot of his bed, where its demon glare gradually faded into the darkness. Had our friend lived two centuries ago, instead of regarding it as an optical illusion, he might have regarded it as a supernatural visitation.

The Wheeling Daily Intelligencer, Wheeling, Virginia [West Virginia], August 30, 1860, pg. 3.

A SPOOK.—An Irish woman, living in the vicinity of the old jail, has several evenings lately seen and conversed with a very ghost, which came stalking into the house like the "goblin damned" in most questionable shape. Night before last, Colonius, the philosopher of the *Staats Zeitung*, without the fear of slung shots and loafers, much less of Spooks, before his eyes, went up in company with others to watch for his ghostship. He gives an item about it, but testifies that, although he watched long and wearily, he saw no ghost. He thinks the whole thing had its origin. He thinks the whole thing had its origin in whisky and recommends lager beer.

The Wheeling Daily Intelligencer, Wheeling, Virginia [West Virginia], December 30, 1862, pg. 3.

A GREAT CIRCULAR GHOST HUNT.—We have heretofore advised our readers that a ghost—a ghastly and horrible ghost—has been perambulating about East Wheeling nearly every night for a couple or three weeks past. Quite a number of persons have seen it and spoken to it and some have thrown stones and brickbats at it. It is a very queer sort of a ghost and seems to have a high regard for its personal comfort. It appears generally about ten o'clock in the evening, with a cowl upon its head like those worn by the members of that ancient and honorable order known as the Sons of Malta.[8] Its person is arrayed in heavy skins and it is said to present a very *outre* appearance.—Recently it has frightened a great many women and children and has got to be a great nuisance in the particular localities which it chooses to infest. Accordingly a party of ten young men organized themselves into a company of ghost hunters on Saturday night and sallied forth to scour the alleys and byways of East Wheeling. Some were armed with pistols, some with pokers, shovels, clubs, stones and other missiles. They divided the company into couples and searched high and low for the ghost, traversing nearly every alley in that quarter of the town. The hunt was altogether unsuccessful. The ghost got wind of the formidable expedition which had been organized for his extermination and appeared in another section of the city much to the terror of the inhabitants thereof.

The truth about this matter is that some bold fellow whose love of fun outruns his judgement and discretion has been playing ghost with wonderful success and those most immediately interested— those whose families have been frightened and annoyed, in some instances with very serious results—have determined to put an end to his prauke. The ghost generally makes his appearance from the neighborhood of the Government stables, near the Hempfield railroad depot.

The Wheeling Daily Intelligencer, Wheeling, Virginia [West Virginia], December 31, 1862, pg. 3.

THE GHOST HUNTERS.—Another large party was out on Monday night hunting the ghost, with the usual success.—The ghost is a more discreet ghost than we supposed. It don't care about being

---

[8] The Independent Order of the Sons of Malta were a fraternal organization popular during the mid-nineteenth century.

beaten with sticks or perforated with bullets. It will doubtless remain in its prison house until the excitement it has created shall subside.

It is the general impression about town that somebody will be hurt before this is done with. A set of fellows when ghosting and garroting around is about played out. There is such a thing as too much of a good thing.

The Wheeling Daily Intelligencer, Wheeling, Virginia [West Virginia], January 1, 1863, pg. 4.

THAT GHOST.—The ghost was seen again on Tuesday evening, and consented to indulge in a conversation with a gentleman who happened to meet him upon the commons. We think that the sooner this ghost is taught a lesson the better it will be for him and the particular locality to which he chooses to circulate.

The Wheeling Daily Intelligencer, Wheeling, Virginia [West Virginia], January 7, 1863, pg. 3.

MORE GHOSTS.—Owing to the sensation created by the East Wheeling ghost other enterprising young men are engaging in the business. There is scarcely a section of the city now but can boast of its ghost. A very remarkable ghost has established his headquarters somewhere on Caldwell's Run, and has selected for his "beat" the plank walk between Hamilton's Foundry and Ritchietown. We very much fear that somebody will receive severe personal injury before this ghosting business is done with.

During the Civil War in Wheeling, Virginia, ghost sightings were frequent. The sightings abruptly stopped after this part of Virginia became part of the new state of West Virginia on July 4, 1863. (Image courtesy of *The Illustrated Police News*).

VOLUME XI.   WHEELING, VA., TUESDAY MORNING, FEBRUARY 17, 1863.   NUMBER 153.

The Wheeling Daily Intelligencer, Wheeling, Virginia [West Virginia], February 17, 1863, pg. 3.

THE GHOST.—We understand that a ghost has lately made its appearance in our neighboring village of Martinsville, and is in the habit of making nocturnal perambulations through the muddy streets of that place. It is thought to be the same ghost who lately distinguished himself in this city.

Michelle L. Hamilton

The Richmond Dispatch, Richmond, Virginia, August 5, 1863, pg. 1.

LOCAL MATTERS.

Playing Ghost.—On Monday night Julius Saul, a sailor in the Confederate services, was shot in the arm while playing ghost for his own amusement of a comrade. It seems that Saul had been attempting to impress upon the mind of a certain landlady in Rocketts that her establishment was haunted, averring that he had himself seen ghosts walking about the premises. The old lady became somewhat uneasy, and secured the services of two young men to watch for the nocturnal visitors. During the night Saul and a comrade, arrayed in spotless white, made their appearance as regular ghosts, and in that capacity attempted to frighten the watchman from their posts. One of them blazed away at the "spirits," and lodged the contents of a pistol in Saul's arm, eliciting a painful flesh wound.

The Richmond Enquirer, Richmond, Virginia, August 7, 1863, pg. 1.

A GHOST STORY.—The inhabitants of a large long, tumbling-down old brick building, which has adorned Rocketts for at least a century, succeeded until Monday night investing their abode with a mystery which excited the nerves of the immediate community to no slight extent, by saying, in short the house was haunted.—They evidently believed their own story, and as they were deemed honest folks, their sincerity was unquestioned. Spirits had rapped at their doors: white things had been seen to flit along the passages, and all that. On Monday night a "committee of investigation" from the neighborhood went into the house and waited for the ghosts. Presently a door was heard creaking, and then a couple of ghosts appeared on the steps; one of the watchers fired a pistol and the ghosts vanished. The "committee," unable to account for this sudden disappearance, and finding no traces of their continued presence on the premises, conceded that they were "real ghosts," and adopted a ghost creed immediately. On yesterday morning, a seaman, named Julius Saul, called on his surgeon with a bullet hole in his shoulder, and told him a strange story about skylarking some old people, with a comrade, on the night before, done in Rocketts, and being taken mistaken for a ghost, "which he was a 'playin,'" he got the wound. On being asked how often he had engaged in such fun, he replied, "all his life." It was an amusement he could'nt resist, especially when the houses were of the right sort for making an impression.

Michelle L. Hamilton

Part III

Reconstruction 1866 - 1876

The Public Ledger, Memphis, Tennessee, March 22, 1866, pg. 1.

About Ghosts.

Nearly all neighborhoods and communities have their ghost legends. There is a locality not far from Charlottesville, which is reputed to be an old Indian burying-ground,[9] where the ghost of an old warrior called Chillis is said to raise the war-whoop and perform other strange antics every night.

While we were rubbing our heads against the walls of the University,[10] a party of adventurous students thought they would investigate the habits of Chilis. So one night they visited his stamping ground. With nervous apprehension and excitement they

[9] The Native American burial mound is now known as Jefferson's Mound Archaeological Site. The mound was located near the Rivanna River, north of Charlottesville in Albemarle County. In 1784, Thomas Jefferson ordered an excavation of the mound and discovered the remains men, women, and children. Jefferson estimated the site was the burial location of an approximately thousand bodies. Today the location of the mound is unknown.

[10] The University of Virginia located in Charlottesville.

approached the spot, and sure enough, they were greeted with something between a whoop and a screech, which proceeded from a white object with horns and feathers upon its head. They took to their heels, of course, but subsequently learned that the source of their terror was the whistling of the wind through the cavities of an old ox's skull, which had been put on the top of a stump.

We believe that most ghosts can be vanquished by a good cudgel or Colt's revolver and the demonstration of sufficient nerve for their employment.—*Richmond Times.*

The Norfolk Virginian, Norfolk, Virginia, November 26, 1866, pg. 2

Papers, North and South, are asserting that J. Wilkes Booth[11] "still lives."—Booth was good as the "Ghost" in Hamlet, and perhaps his spirit, if he be really dead, is making a professional tour of the earth in his favorite character.

The Alexandria Gazette, Alexandria, Virginia, January 25, 1867, pg. 1.

Gen. Robert E. Lee's Estate.
[Washington Cor. of the St. Louis Times.]

The stranger in Washington, down Louisiana avenue with his face to the west, sees before him, when he gets to the front of the City Hall, on the south side of the Potomac, and on a commanding

---

[11] Actor John Wilkes Booth (1838-1865) assassinated President Abraham Lincoln on April 14, 1865. Tracked down at a farmhouse in Caroline County, Virginia, Booth by the Union army, Booth was killed by Sgt. Boston Corbett on April 26, 1865. Despite his remains being identified by associates, theories persist that Booth somehow eluded capture and lived out his life under an assumed name in Texas and Oklahoma. Booth was a popular Shakespearean actor best known for his performance as Hamlet.

eminence, an edifice which, at the distance of three miles from the point of vision, resembles a Greek temple. This is Arlington House, the residence before the war, of General Robert E. Lee.[12] The Arlington estate was one of the largest, handsomest, and most valuable in the State of Virginia. At an early period of the war the mansion was stripped of everything valuable that could be carried away by the soldiers from Pennsylvania and New England. Pictures, mirrors, statuary, rare and costly books, old china and silver plate, were all gobbled up, and sent off to the "loyal" North. These articles are now to be seen in dozens of houses in the States I have named.

A faithful negro servant,[13] who had remained on the place, saw this stealing going on day after day, and at last came over to the city, got one of the servants of the White House to secure him an interview with Abraham Lincoln; laid the facts before him, and begged him not to permit "Massa Robert's" property to be thus despoiled. Mr. Lincoln's reply, in substance, was said to be that he could not interfere with the military; that the soldiers were only doing at Arlington what they soon would do all over the South; and that as for Bob Lee, he was a traitor, and had no rights which the soldiers were bound to respect. The result was that the house and grounds were soon made to look like the abomination of desolation.

---

[12] Arlington House was completed in 1818 by George Washington Parke Custis (1781-1857) as a shrine to his step-grandfather George Washington. In 1831, Custis' only daughter Mary Custis married Robert E. Lee. During the Civil War, Arlington House was confiscated by the federal government for unpaid taxes.

[13] This account about an unnamed male enslaved worker meeting with President Lincoln to protect the personal possessions of the Lee family is fictional. When Mary Lee left Arlington House in the spring of 1861, she left the keys to the mansion to her personal maid Selina Grey. Salina Grey was born at Arlington House and was an enslaved worker of the Custis and Lee family. When Arlington House was commandeered by Union forces in May 1861, officers began to loot the mansion, taking as souvenirs items that had belonged to George and Martha Washington. The thefts stopped after Salina Grey complained to Union Gen. Irvin McDowell, who had the remaining Washington artifacts moved to the Patent Office in Washington, D.C.

Finally, the Government went to work and buried the bodies of 16,000 white soldiers on one side of the house, and the bodies of 1,600 negro soldiers on the other.[14] It is said that the negroes who live in that vicinity frighten their children by telling them the most frightful ghost stories about these dead bodies.

They say that every night at midnight the ghosts of these 1,600 negro soldiers rise from their graves and dance a Virginia break-down on the graves of their 16,000 white comrades; and that the ghosts of the latter, thus unceremoniously disturbed, arise likewise, and attack the black ghosts; that the fight rages between the black and white ghosts till 1 A. M., when the black ghosts prevail (one black ghost being more than a match for ten white ones,) and drive the white ghosts howling to their sepulchers, when they finish their break-down, and then vanish to their own graves.

A colony of several hundred blacks was established by the Government on another part of the estate, and they were provided with comfortable huts, furniture, utensils, implements, etc., and were then told to go to work.[15] Not one obeyed out of ten. The other nine stole and sold everything they could carry off, and spent their time in idleness. Now that the winter is here, they are suffering from hunger and cold, and the people of Washington have been appealed to to save them from perishing. How much better to have left them to their kind masters?

A. D.

---

[14] These were the first burials of what would become Arlington National Cemetery.

[15] The Arlington Freedmen's Village was established as a refugee camp for the region's freed enslaved workers. Though the Freedmen's Village was meant to be a temporary facility, a thriving community was established and remained active until 1900.

The Edgefield Advertiser, Edgefield, South Carolina, February 13, 1867, pg. 1.

A GHOST.—A day or two since, a gentleman employed one of the grave diggers at Hollywood to disinter the remains of a friend who had been buried there. The work was commenced in the afternoon, and dark came on before it was completed. The grave digger was remunerated and put the money in his pocket book in his pocket. He returned to his lodgings, smoked his pipe and went to bed. After getting in bed it struck him that he did not feel his pocket book in the pocket of his breeches when he pulled them off. He immediately got up, and finding that he was right in the matter, threw a blanket over his shoulders, and without putting on his clothes, went to the grave where he had been at work, and made search for his lost money. He got down on his hands and felt on the ground for it.

Just at this time a party of Yankee soldiers,[16] who had been using the road through the cemetery as a near cut from their camp to the city, came along. The grave digger heard them coming and as they got to the fence, gave an unearthly groan. This attracted their attention, and looking in the direction from which the sound proceeded, they espied a white object moving about amongst the graves. They halted. Another groan. They turned to flee, when the foremost of the party, who had gotten on top of the fence, got his drapery entangled on the palings, and in his frantic efforts to get down, left about half a yard of sky-blue cloth from the rear portion of his pants on top of the fence. They made telegraph time back to camp, and will doubtless take the other road to the city in future, when they come in the night time.—Richmond Times.

---

[16] During Reconstruction, Union troops occupied Virginia.

Michelle L. Hamilton

VOLUME LXVIII.   ALEXANDRIA VA. WEDNESDAY EVENING, OCTOBER 30, 1867.   NUMBER 254

The Alexandria Gazette, Alexandria, Virginia, October 30, 1867, pg. 2.

A GHOST STORY.—They have a Ghost, or *something* in Albemarle, which appears to be decidedly a "run 'un." His ghostship is impervious to minnies,[17] pistol balls, and such, and regards them no more than if they were fired into the air, instead of at his "spirit majesty." The theatre of his operations is the dwelling house of Mr. John S. Moon[18], a prominent citizen, living near Scottsville, and the story goes that the Ghost has visited the premises for upwards of thirty consecutive nights, up to last Wednesday, the latest accounts we have from him. The house has been under a strong armed guard for the most of this time, and yet the Ghost eludes them, and passes into the building either through the door, or the windows as may suit his fancy. As we have stated, it regards not bullets, having been repeatedly fired at without effect, with the muzzles of the guns almost touching *its* breast. Amid a

A GHOST STORY.—They have a Ghost, or *something* in Albemarle, which appears to be decidedly a "rum 'un." His ghostship is impervious to minnies, pistol balls, and such, and regards them no more than if they were fired into the thin air, instead of at his "spirit majesty." The theatre of his operations is the dwelling house of Mr. John S. Moon, a prominent citizen, living near Scottsville, and the story goes that the Ghost has visited the premises for upwards of thirty consecutive nights, up to last Wednesday, the latest accounts we have from him. The house has been under a strong armed guard for the most of this time, and yet the Ghost eludes them, and passes into the building either through the door, or the windows as may suit his fancy. As we have stated, it regards not bullets, having been repeatedly fired at without effect, with the muzzles of the guns almost touching *its* breast. Amid a storm of balls the ghost walks about as unconcernedly as if there were no other *person* beside himself in the word, visits all parts of the house, and when he is satisfied, walks away. His ghostship, it appears, is not above handling carnal weapons, for on Monday or Tuesday night of last week, a Miss Tompkins, an inmate of the house, fired twice at *him* with a pistol, and the fire was returned, Miss T. being struck in the forehead with the ball from

---

[17] The Minié ball or Minie ball were designed to be loaded into an American Springfield Model 1861 or a British Pattern 1853 Enfield rifled musket and was used to devastating effect during the Civil War.

[18] John Schuyler Moon (1823-1876) was a prominent lawyer in Albemarle County. Moon married Elizabeth Thompkins (1826-1891) in 1847 and the couple had fourteen children. The hauntings occurred at the Moon family home, Church Hill, which had been purchased as a summer residence before the Civil War.

storm of balls the ghost walks about as unconcernedly as if there were no other *person* beside himself in the word, visits all parts of the house, and when he is satisfied, walks away. His ghostship, it appears, is not above handling carnal weapons, for on Monday or Tuesday night of last week, a Miss Tompkins, an inmate of the house, fired twice at *him* with a pistol, and the fire was returned, Miss T being struck in the forehead with the ball from his weapon, but not much hurt. His ghostship has been seen by numbers beside Mr. Moon and his family, nearly all of whom have had a shot at him, but without effect.—He is described as a large *man* well-dressed and *black*. Our last bulletin from the scene of the perambulations of this visitor from the spirit land was up to Wednesday night. The neighborhood was then in a high state of excitement, and the house of Mr. Moon was guarded inside and out by a dozen or more armed men who had determined to capture the ghost at all hazards. Whether they have succeeded we are not prepared to say.— *Lynchburg News.*

The Moon family home called Church Hill became the center of a mysterious haunting that occurred from 1867 to 1868. (Image courtesy of Findagrave.com).

The Staunton Spectator, Staunton, Virginia, November 5, 1867, pg. 3.

THE ALBEMARLE GHOST.

The citizens of Albemarle are greatly exercised about a mysterious personage (or what seems to be such) which has been visiting nightly, for five or six weeks, the house of Mr. Jno. S. Moon, a respectable citizen, living near Scottsville. All efforts to kill or capture it have proved fruitless, though the house has been guarded by a number of brave armed men, who have frequently shot at it. It appears and goes through the house at will, and does not regard the shots from guns and pistols. The Lynchburg *News* says that a reward of $500[19] has been offered by the citizens for either the capture or killing of it, whatever it may be, or for a satisfactory explanation of the phenomenon.

The Alexandria Gazette, Alexandria, Virginia, November 6, 1867, pg. 4.

THE ALBEMARLE GHOST.—The remarkable visits to the house of John S. Moon, esq., near Scottsville, are still going on. Sunday night the powerful light so frequently seen, flooded the passage of the house, and was subsequently seen from the upper windows lighting up the night. These visits have been going on now *four months*. The house has been entered certainly ten or fifteen times, and probably much oftener. For the first two months the visits averaged once in ten days; for the last two months, they have averaged several times a week. Mr. Moon's house has been guarded now for, perhaps, a month; but it seems impossible to capture the mysterious strangers, who enter the house right in the midst of the

---

[19] Approximately $9,267.23 in 2021.

circle of pickets. The parties (it is supposed there are three of them) carry false keys, and open out-doors and in-doors; they have also a shrill whistle which as been repeatedly heard; and they have a very remarkable lantern which is often seen.—*Charlottesville Chronicle*.

The Norfolk Virginia, Norfolk, Virginia, November 8, 1867, pg. 3.

The *Chronicle* says: The "Ghosts" continue to visit the house of Mr. John S. Moon, near Scottsville.... A party of students from the University[20] went out there Wednesday night.

The Native Virginian, Orange, Virginia, November 15, 1867, pg. 2.

THE GHOST.—The house of Mr. John S. Moon is still being assailed. For the past week the house has been stoned. Nobody caught.

The Richmond Dispatch, Richmond, Virginia, November 28, 1867, pg. 1.

THE ALBEMARLE GHOST NOT CAUGHT.—The scoundrel who has been annoying Mr. John S. Moon, of Albemarle, by his ghostly exhibitions had not been arrested as late as Tuesday, 26th instant, as we are informed by a letter received on yesterday from Mr. Moon. The scamp had become even more violent in his demonstrations, as on his last visit he threw stones into the house, smashing the glass and doing other damage. From all we can learn,

---

[20] The University of Virginia in Charlottesville.

we believe such steps have now been taken as will soon stop his diabolical proceedings and bring him and his abettors to punishment.

The Alexandria Gazette, Alexandria, Virginia, November 29, 1867, pg. 2.

The Richmond Enquirer has learned that the "Ghost" on the farm of Mr. Moon, in Albemarle, has been found out, it having been definitely ascertained that the "ghost" was a negro with a magic lantern, who had been employed by a party who wished to buy the farm, to frighten the family off of it, with the hope he might get it for a small sum. The "Cock Lane Ghost"[21] is beaten in all respects by this enterprising would-be dealer in real estate.—[But there is doubt thrown over the discovery; for the Richmond Dispatch says the imposture was not discovered up to the 26th instant; but steps were being taken to clear up the mystery.]

The Native Virginian, Orange, Virginia, November 29, 1867, pg. 3.

THE ALBEMARLE GHOST.—A gentleman from Nelson, reported here last week that the ghost had been caught and lodged in the Charlottesville jail. But the Scottsville Register, the organ of the ghost, says:—Since the 11th, his majesty, the devil, or his emissary, has been making his usual visits. On Saturday night last

---

[21] The Cock Lane Ghost was a notorious haunting in Cock Lane in London in 1762. The haunting centered on the ghost of Fanny Lynes who claimed that she had been murdered by her husband. The ghost of Fanny Lynes became a media sensation and was reveled to be a hoax.

he was shot at twice, but he escaped by 'running like a deer.' On last night he simply threw his light about the premises.

For the last few nights he threw his light about the premises. On Wednesday evening he was seen about dusk.

Mr. Moon offers $500 reward for his apprehension.

DAILY DISPATCH.

VOL. XXXIII.   RICHMOND, THURSDAY MORNING, DECEMBER 5, 1867.   NO. 155

The Richmond Dispatch, Richmond, Virginia, December 5, 1867, pg. 4.

From our Special Reporter.

THE ALBEMARLE GHOST.
THE MYSTERY STILL UNSOLVED.
Further Particulars Concerning his Mysterious Majesty.
RESUME OF THE FACTS IN THE CASE.

SCOTTSVILLE, VA., December 2, 1867.

The interest manifested in the mysterious manifestations at the residence of J. S. Moon, Esq., is still unabated. The report that the author of the disturbances has been discovered and arrested is utterly without foundation. For a period of nearly ten months Mr. Moon's residence has been occasionally haunted by the mysterious stranger or strangers; but it is unnecessary here to enter into a detail of the circumstances, as the *Dispatch* has already furnished its readers with the principal facts in the case.

The first question is now asked of any one coming from Mr. Moon's neighborhood are, "What is the news from Mr. Moon's? Was the rogue there last night?" His last decided demonstration was on last Tuesday night, when he threw a few stones as the house. The cause of his suspending his operations for long a time is supposed to be the fact that he has recently had special reasons to fear detection. What these reasons are it would not now be prudent to disclose. To publish them might lessen the chances of detecting the bold perpetrators of these singular annoyances. Beside suspicion may now rest on an innocent man.

It is certainly a very strange affair.—We call "the thing" a rogue; and yet, if a rogue at all, he is only a rogue in a very small way. He has had many opportunities to take things of value, but one or two pounds of sugar and coffee, a few small articles of clothing, and two or three loads of powder and shot, are all that he is supposed to have taken. It is out of the question to suppose that he wishes to do Mr. Moon a personal injury, as he might do this at

From our Special Reporter.

THE ALBEMARLE GHOST.

THE MYSTERY STILL UNSOLVED.

Further Particulars Concerning his Mysterious Majesty.

RESUME OF THE FACTS IN THE CASE.

SCOTTSVILLE, VA., December 2, 1867.
The interest manifested in the mysterious manifestations at the residence of J. S. Moon, Esq., is still unabated. The report that the author of the disturbances has been discovered and arrested is utterly without foundation. For a period of nearly ten months Mr. Moon's residence has been occasionally haunted by the mysterious stranger or strangers; but it is unnecessary here to enter into a detail of the circumstances, as the *Dispatch* has already furnished its readers with the principal facts in the case.

any time. Nor yet is it probable that he is influenced by feelings of hostility toward any member of the family. That he should expose his life night after night simply "for the fun of the thing" is almost inconceivable. What then, can be his motive? The future may reveal.

Those who have had the best opportunities of knowing all the facts of the case suppose that at least three persons have been engaged in it. Only one, however, has ever been seen at a time. There is a tall figure and a low figure, and another of which nothing is known. The tall figure, we believe, is the most daring. He is specially noted for throwing lights about. These lights are of two kinds. One is an ordinary light, which might be thrown from any lamp or lantern, and the other is described as of a very singular character. It comes into a room through a thick curtain, and shows itself in a round spot not much larger than a silver dollar, illuminating only the spot upon which it rests. It does not remain long in one place, but dances about with the utmost agility. A lady who has seen it frequently remarked that it is the most curious light she ever saw, impressing her with the belief that it was supernatural. These lights are thrown into persons' faces, and never fail to blind them for the time.

That "the thing" should have escaped detection and injury is a matter of great surprise. Many of the gentlemen who have watched for him are men of tried coolness and courage; and some of those who have shot at him are both brave men and excellent marksmen. One, we know, as reliable man as ever guarded a picket post, had a fire at him at short range, but the shot was without effect. The supposition, however, that all the guards thought "the thing" a ghost is incorrect. Whatever they may have thought before, they are inclined to believe that he is a man, since he fired at Mrs. Moon's sister. Spiritual agencies do not use such carnal weapons as powder and ball. He has been shot at some twenty times, and, as far as known, has never received the slightest hurt. Some who have shot at him have thought they heard him laugh aloud as he ran off.

It has now been more than two months since "the thing" has been visiting Mr. Moon's premises regularly night after night. It made occasional visits all through the spring and summer. It has rocked his house, thrown strange lights into his windows, battered his doors, broken his window glass, got upon his house, rattled his door locks, and played sundry other pranks, even while the house and yard were all guarded, and yet has failed to be caught. We hazard nothing is saying it is the boldest, silliest, most successful thing of the kind that ever was played in Virginia.

Your reporter proposes to remain in the neighborhood in order to keep the readers of the *Dispatch* fully posted concerning everything that transpires. Great care will be taken that no unreliable reports or more sensational rumors are forwarded.

ENDOR.

The Native Virginian, Orange, Virginia, December 13, 1867, pg. 3.

THE MOON HOAX.—A friend assures us that the "Albemarle Ghost" is all a joke, gotten up by that wag, Brady, who edits the Scottsville Register, for the sake of attracting attention to his little town. The Mr. Moon, a lawyer, is in fact the man in the moon. Can this be true?

The Staunton Spectator, Staunton, Virginia, December 24, 1867, pg. 2.

The Albemarle "ghost" has not made its appearance for three weeks, and strong hopes are entertained that the nuisance has been permanently abated.

The Alexandria Gazette, Alexandria, Virginia, December 26, 1867, pg. 2.

The Albemarle Ghost re-appeared a few nights ago, at Mr. Moon's residence, playing tricks, opening doors, &c. The house is guarded, but the "ghost" seems always to deceive the sentinels, and glide in and out, at pleasure. "Rest, perturbed spirit, rest!" But, if they should catch the ghost, what a time there will be!

The Native Virginian.

BY BAGBY & STOFER. }   *Patriæ fumat, ipse alimæ, lucidator*   { TERMS—$3.00 IN ADVANCE.

VOLUME 1.   ORANGE COURT HOUSE, VA., FRIDAY MORNING, JANUARY 3, 1868.   NUMBER 7.

The Native Virginian, Orange, Virginia, January 3, 1868, pg. 3.

ANOTHER MOON GHOST.—One muddy night, during Christmas week, while we were in the country, mysterious noises were heard over the house—doors opening, hollow sounds inside the walls, hoarse voices in the yard, strange growling, and, above all, the ringing of the back-door bell, which had not been heard for years. At intervals, all night long, this bell was heard. The sleep of the household was broken, and many were the speculations, at the breakfast table next morning, as to the cause of these queer noises, especially the bell-ringing. It could not have been the wind, because there had been much windier nights, and the bell had never stirred. Just as we had reached the conclusion that the Moon ghost had emigrated from Albemarle, a young gentleman, who had gone to examine into the matter, returned and reported that the old black hen had selected the

ANOTHER MOON GHOST.—One muddy night, during Christmas week, while we were in the country, mysterious noises were heard over the house—doors opening, hollow sounds inside the walls, hoarse voices in the yard, strange growling, and, above all, the ringing of the back-door bell, which had not been heard for years. At intervals, all night long, this bell was heard. The sleep of the household was broken, and many were the speculations, at the breakfast table next morning, as to the cause of these queer noises, especially the bell-ringing. It could not have been the wind, because there had been much windier nights, and the bell had never stirred. Just as we had reached the conclusion that the Moon ghost had emigrated from Albemarle, a young gentleman, who had gone to examine into the matter, returned and reported that the old black hen had selected the transom, close by the bell, as a lodging place for the night. *Hinc Mae lachrymae!*

transom, close by the bell, as a lodging place for the night. *Hinc Mae lachrymae!*[22]

The Alexandria Gazette, Alexandria, Virginia, February 5, 1868, pg. 2.

THE ALBEMARLE GHOST.—The Scottsville *Register* of the 1st says:

"Sometime back we gave a detailed account in the *Register* of what "the Ghost" had been doing up to a certain date. Some of our exchanges and some of our readers look upon the whole affair as a "miserable hoax," but we can assure them they are mistaken. We have taken particular pains to give an unvarnished history of the movements of "the Ghost." Gentleman of integrity, and gentlemen of as much intelligence and bravery as "Old Hickory,"[23] have, night after night, for months made unsuccessful efforts to kill or detect the party, or parties that annoy the family of Mr. Moon by throwing lights on and through the house—throwing rocks on the house, and at the guard—getting on the roof and rapping, and knocking out glass—sometimes entering the house with false keys, &c., &c. For sometime past he has failed to throw his light about the premises. We think it more than probable that he has broken his magic lantern.[24] He has not, however, failed, for the past two weeks, to appear in some shape almost every night. Mr. Moon is now on a professional trip South, and since he left, Mr. "Ghost," cuts up more capers than usual, he raps against the house, gets on the roof, (a story

---

[22] *Hinc illae lacrimea* is Latin for "that is what those tears were for."

[23] "Old Hickory" was the nickname for President Andrew Jackson (1767-1845). According to legend, Jackson investigated the Bell Witch haunting in Adams, Tennessee.

[24] A magic lantern was an early image projector. During the 19th-century magic lantern shows were popular forms of entertainment.

and a half high,) and when the guard approach him, he, like the Irishman's flea,[25] "is not there."

The Richmond Dispatch, Richmond, Virginia, March 3, 1868, pg. 3.

The Albemarle Ghost.

From the Scottsville Register.

One chap has been kicking up a terrible rumpus for some three weeks past at Mr. Moon's residence—sometimes two make their appearance. The fact that two have been present lately at the same time is evident from the fact that heavy rapping was heard one night on either side of the house (front and rear) at the same time. Glass has been knocked out and rocks thrown into the house, and the family annoyed in various ways almost nightly for some time past.

A few nights since a man made his appearance; the guard inside had a full view of him. They determined, instead of firing upon him, to open the door suddenly, and try, if possible, to seize him. They therefore threw open the door, and sprang toward him. As quick as thought he gave a dodge, was around the corner, and out of sight. They might as well try to catch a deer.

This is one of the strangest affairs on record. The house has been guarded for a year. One or two men during this time have been seen or heard in and about the house above hundreds of times annoying the family. They have been shot at repeatedly. Indeed, one of them has as much daring as it is possible for any human being to possess. The escapes from death he has made, and is still making, are mysterious and almost miraculous.

Another mystery is, What can be the object of these visits? Why should a man, night after night, the coldest weather imaginable for

---

[25] "The Irishman's Flea" was an 19th-century humorous story about an Irishman that was plagued by fleas.

this climate, expose himself, sometimes to the pelting storm—
sometimes in snow six inches deep? Can it be gratifying to him to
alarm the ladies by rapping, throwing lights, knocking out glass, and
walking over the house occasionally? He must be a despicably mean
creature to wish thus to interrupt innocent (sickly) and unoffending
females. Mr. Moon has been absent more than a month, and it seems
"the ghost" takes more pains since he left to annoy the family than
when he was at home. We would infer from this that it is not Mr.
Moon against whom he has particular spite. We have conversed
with no one that seems to have any fixed opinion on the subject.

Plunder cannot be his object; it cannot be murder. If he wishes
to alarm Mr. Moon's family sufficiently to induce Mr. M. to sell his
farm, he must be deficient in common sense if he expects to
accomplish his object by playing "ghost." We doubt if anyone save
the mysterious fellow himself can account for such strange
proceedings.

The Alexandria Gazette, Alexandria, Virginia, March 11, 1868, pg. 2.

The Scottsville Register, organ of the Moon ghost, says that Mr.
Moon has returned to his home from the South, and that since his
return the goblin has played but few pranks.

The Richmond Dispatch, Richmond, Virginia, March 18, 1868, pg. 3.

THE AFFAIR AT THE RESIDENCE OF MR. J. S. MOON.—
The Scottsville *Register* says that a cowardly miscreant, laying aside
the character of ghost, undertook to play, theatrically, the *rôle* of
assassin at the residence of Mr. Moon on Sunday last about the

middle of the day, in the absence of both Mr. Moon and his eldest son.

The Alexandria Gazette, Alexandria, Virginia, March 25, 1868, pg. 2.

The Scottsville Register says that another "ghost" has made its appearance at the house of a prominent gentleman in Fluvanna, the exploits of which are as mysterious and daring as those of the Albemarle "spirit."

The Spirit of Jefferson, Charles Town, West Virginia, March 31, 1868, pg. 3.

FLUVANNA "GHOST!"—Demonstrations similar to those made at the residence of Mr. Moon have, during the present week, been made at the house of a prominent gentleman in Fluvanna, two or three miles from Scottsville. We can, however, state that nothing has occurred at the residence of Mr. Moon to excel in daring and impudence the course pursued by the "Ghost" and his dog in "Old Flu," on Wednesday night last. The house of the gentleman was entered with false keys, and the chamber, in which he and his sick wife had retired for the night, was entered by some unknown person accompanied by a dog. As soon as a light was struck the ghostly gentleman left the premises, having made no response to questions asked, and taking nothing with him as far as known.—It was his second visit.—*Charlottesville Chron.*

The *Alexandria Gazette*, Alexandria, Virginia, April 1, 1868, pg. 2.

Somebody at Duffield's Depot, in Jefferson country, is endeavoring to imitate the Moon Ghost in Albemarle. It is thought plunder is the object.

The *Progress-Index*, Petersburg, Virginia, April 3, 1868, pg. 3.

TERRIBLE.—Two policemen were placed on special duty at Blandford Cemetery last night. It is terrible to think of such a thing, but we very much fear they have "gone up." Ghosts will walk about grave yards, so they say.

The *Progress-Index*, Petersburg, Virginia, April 4, 1868, pg. 3.

SAFE.—We felt considerably relieved yesterday morning, when, on making enquiry, we were informed of the bodily safety of the two policemen who had been assigned to special duty at Blandford Cemetery the night previous; and we were, therefore, more resigned to the assignment of others there late night.—The fact is, there is no "Moon Ghost" about the Old Church, and ordinary ghosts only venture about on bright moonlight nights. We do not know what may turn up when the moon [is] full.

The Old Blandford Church in Blandford Cemetery.
(Image courtesy of Wikipedia).

The Progress-Index, Petersburg, Virginia, April 6, 1868, pg. 2.

The Wytheville "Dispatch" announced that a veritable ghost has made its appearance in that town, and nearly frightened out of his wits one Capt. Barnett, a man of heroic mould, who beheld the said goblin in a lonely and deserted house.

The Richmond Dispatch, Richmond, Virginia, April 7, 1868, pg. 2.

THE ALBEMARLE GHOST SUBSIDES.—A letter received in this city states that a week or ten days ago each of the householders living within a circuit of several miles about Mr. Moon's residence were individually warned that they would render themselves liable to suspicion and arrest it they were absent from home on a certain night. The ghost had before been active, and it was supposed had opened the spring campaign. Upon that night it was not visible, and there have been no manifestations of his Satanic Majesty's presence since. A certain white man in the neighborhood is supposed, with good reason, to be at the bottom of the affair, and he is now under strict surveillance. So says the letter-writer, who is in a position to know.

The Staunton Spectator, Staunton, Virginia, July 7, 1868, pg. 4.

Albemarle Ghost.

About two months since we were in Frederick county, Va. We there met with Mr. Abraham Myers, who seemed to take a great deal of interest in the Moon Ghost. He was an intelligent (though we think somewhat eccentric) gentleman. He spoke earnestly and fluently on the subject, and averred that if the three last chapters of Daniel[26] were read aloud on the premises the "Ghost" would disappear, at least for a time. On our return home we made this known. The chapters were read and the Ghost ceased operations; but within the past few days he has commenced in full blast—knocking out windows and acting as badly and as fearlessly as ever.

Mr. Myers, who is a wealthy gentleman, requested us, in case the Ghost returned, to inform him, and he would come over and silence him forever. Of course, "the honor and glory" of dispensing with the Ghost's services for all time will compensate Mr. M.

---

[26] Chapters 10-12 of the Book of Daniel in the Old Testament of the Bible describes the prophet Daniel's final visions. The prophet foresees a conflict between an unnamed "King of the North" and the "King of the South" which will herald the beginning of the "time of the end" when Israel will be victorious, and the dead will be raised.

without any extra charge. We shall look for him.—*Scottsville Register*.

The National Republican.

VOL. 8—NO. 202.   WASHINGTON, D. C., WEDNESDAY, JULY 22, 1868.   PRICE 3 CENTS.

The National Republican, Washington, D. C., July 22, 1868, pg. 2.

The Memorial Association of Manassas.

We are in receipt of the following communication from Manassas, Va., which we publish as received, that our readers may notice the spirit that yet pervades the hearts of our Southern neighbors. We, however, approve of these people taking care of the remains of their unfortunate dead. It shows a commendable spirit:

MANASSAS, July 21, 1868.

...In the meantime, however, Walter Weir, esq., a prominent lawyer of this county, was introduced to the large assemblage of ladies and gentlemen by Major W. W. Thornton, and delivered a very able and interesting address as follows:

LADIES AND GENTLEMEN: ...

We all remember well, it was on such a day as this, seven long, weary years ago, that a noble Southern band, battling for the right, offered up their lives on the plains of Manassas. To-day is the anniversary of that fearful day; that day of wrath. And to-day, methinks the sad and mournful ghosts of that noble band of soldiers rise before us. They come and point their ghostly fingers at us, and cry out for rest! Their bodies lie scattered and bleaching on the dismal plains of Manassas. They are weary, and have no resting place; there is no home for the dead. The summer suns are hot and fierce, the wintry winds are cold and cheerless. They tell us of the glory of the past and the happy hours that once smiled on them. They whisper to us of shattered hearthstones and broken hearts....

The Richmond Dispatch, Richmond, Virginia, July 28, 1868, pg. 3.

"ALBEMARLE GHOST."—The "ghost," with but few exceptions, makes his nightly appearance at the residence of Mr. Moon. We do not like to allude to the mysterious affair, but as a public journalist it is our duty to do so. There is nothing in the annals of history so mysterious to us as the performance of the "ghost." It does not surprise us to hear of rocks flying through windows and of flashing lights; but it does not only surprise but astonishes us to know that for the past two years the greatest effort has been made to detect the rogue or "ghost," and he is still defying the guard and playing his pranks as usual. Mr. Myers must come over and "read the three last chapters of Daniel."—*Scottsville Register*.

The Alexandria Gazette, Alexandria, Virginia, July 31, 1868, pg. 2.

A "Ghost" has made its appearance in that part of Richmond called Butchertown, and frightened the people of the house where it "appeared." It turned out to be a live woman!

The "Albemarle Ghost," with but few exceptions, makes his nightly appearance at the residence of Mr. Moon. No detection has yet been made.

DAILY DISPATCH.

VOL. XXXV.   RICHMOND, MONDAY MORNING, AUGUST 24, 1868.   NO. 47.

The Richmond Dispatch, Richmond, Virginia, August 24, 1868, pg. 4.

LETTER FROM ALBEMARLE.
Correspondent of the Richmond Dispatch.
Pleasant Trip—Latest Freaks of the Albemarle Ghost…

HOWARDSVILLE, August 21, 1868.

General Mahone has worked a wonderful reformation in the management of the Virginia and Tennessee railroad, and Mr. Vandegrift has always kept the Lynchburg and Charlottesville line in apple-pie order; so the trip from Bonsacks to this point is very comfortable and pleasant, rendered the more so at this time by the refreshing rains which have settled the dust and crowned the hills and valleys with splendid corn or fresh and beautiful grass.

We are now in the region of the famous "Albemarle ghost," and have heard many stories concerning his antics. His visits have recently been frequent and violent—throwing rocks against the house and into the windows, yelling at midnight around the house, etc., but several nights since he left a note—written in large capitals and signed "Ghost"—in which he promises the family not to disturb them again. Whether this was written in good faith or is a mere trick to put the family off their guard remains to be seen. No clue to the perpetrator of these outrages has yet been discovered, but Mr. Moon's family are so thoroughly convinced that the disturbance comes from *earthly* visitants that they are not at all superstitious about the matter, but are still on the alert in the hope of bringing the miscreants to deserved punishment.

Michelle L. Hamilton

The *Alexandria Gazette*, Alexandria, Virginia, August 29, 1868, pg. 1.

The "Albemarle Ghost."
[From the Native Virginian]

Within sight of "Plaindealing" and about three hundred yards from the road, is the now famous house of Mr. Moon, where "the Albemarle ghost" has played his strange and daring pranks for over eighteen months. I got out of the ambulance and walked through the woods to take a good look at the house. It is situated some hundred and fifty yards from the woods, with nothing within that distance to obstruct the view on any side, and hence the great wonder that the rascal or rascals were able to carry on their pranks for so long a time without detection, and that too in defiance of often times from ten to twenty guards around the house. It is a notable fact, however, that whenever the students from the University came down, as they frequently did in large numbers, the "ghost" never made his appearance.

My opinion was, when I first read the account published a few months ago in the Scottsville Register, that the "ghost" was somebody who lived in the house or in the servant's quarters. Mr. Moon, whose acquaintance I had made in Charlottesville a year ago, and with whom I met in Scottsville, tells me that he believes negroes and perhaps some white men belonging to a band a horse thieves scattered through the neighborhood, to be at the bottom of this mischief. He showed me, however, a note which he had found tied to a fishing pole in his front porch a few days before. It read thus:— "I will not pester you any more Mr. Jack. GHOST!"

He thought this note, which was printed with a pencil in capital letters, came from a negro, because "Mr. or Master Jack" was the name given him by the negroes when he was a small boy, and because the J. in Jack was turned the wrong way."

And an examination of the note, I could not agree with him. It was written on very small note paper, ornamented with a flowered border in purple ink. Most of the letters were far too well executed to have come from the clumsy hand of a negro, who had recently been taught to write. Turning the J the wrong way was an after thought of the writer as he or she was writing the last word, and intended to mislead. "Ghost" was spelt correctly, but that Mr. Moon attributed to the fact that the negroes had so often seen the word printed in the Scottsville Register. But to me the conclusive part of the evidence was this: After the writer had finished writing in capital letters the words given above, there remained a long space between GHOST and the lower part of the purple flowered border. A portion was then cut out and the lower portion of the border *pinned* to the upper and larger piece of paper, so that the border just enclosed neatly the promise, "I will not pester you any more Mr. Jack. Ghost."

The conclusion to my mind was irresistible, that the writer of the note was a woman, a white woman, and an educated woman. The "ghost" had kept the promise so far and had not disturbed Mr. Moon since the night on which the note was left, nevertheless Mr. M. said that, much as he had been annoyed, he would rather the ghost would keep up his (or her) tricks until caught and properly punished.

The Richmond Dispatch, Richmond, Virginia, September 4, 1868, pg. 3.

THE MOON GHOST.—It is rumored over here that Mr. Moon is his own ghost, and that he enjoys the fun hugely.—*Valley Virginian.*

Michelle L. Hamilton

The Richmond Dispatch, Richmond, Virginia, September 25, 1868, pg. 4.

REV. DR. BOND ON PLANCHETTE.—Planchette is one of the several modern necromantic inventions through which weak-minded ghosts or other intellectually feeble incorporeal are mechanically assisted to communicate with human stupidity, and mingle the thinner imbecilities of a disembodied world with the grosser ignorance of this. The instrument, constructed for simpletons, is properly very simple.

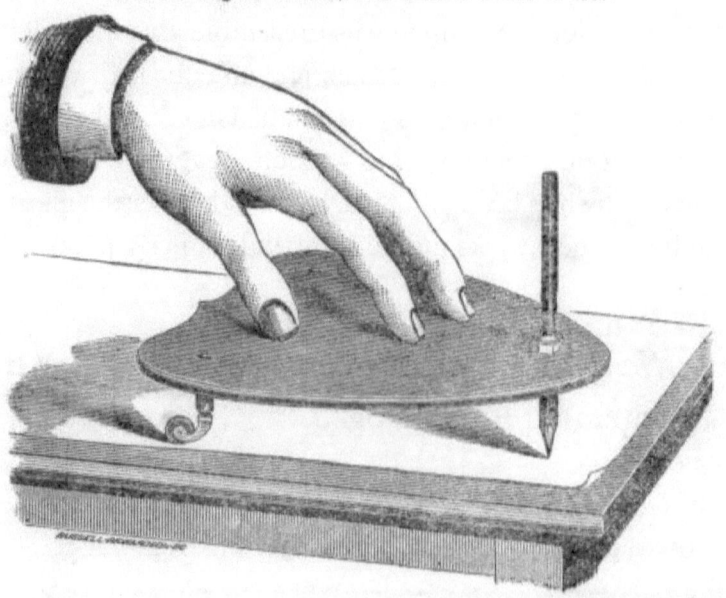

Ad for a planchette c. 1860. (Image courtesy Wikipedia).

The Shepherdstown Register, Shepherdstown, West Virginia, October 17, 1868, pg. 2.

A GHOST IN ROANOKE COUNTY, VA.—A correspondent of the Lynchburg Republican says:

"Great excitement is prevailing in Roanoke county. The mysterious phenomena, which have so often appeared in Albemarle county, have at last visited us. The report is altogether credible, having been related first in town yesterday morning by several reliable citizens living in the immediate vicinity of Mr. J. M. Barker, three miles northwest of Salem, who is now the victim of its nightly incursions. Whether there be any relationship existing between this family and that of Mr. Moon, that he should now be made the object of its persecutions, we know not. Its conduct has been such as to warrant the belief that it is identical with the phenomena which have so long disturbed the quiet of the Moon family. It first appeared to a black man, crossing a field in the direction of Mr. Barker's house, walking so rapidly from a skirt of woods across the field as if to intercept him. The negro, being much frightened, rapidly advanced to the house, where Mrs. Barker, with her two daughters, was remaining during the absence of her husband in town. Scarcely had the house been secured when its tread was heard upon the porch, and rocks were hurled upon the porch, and rocks were hurled upon the roof and against the blinds. Soon a flood of light poured into the house, as if coming from beneath the window outside. Nothing was heard of it after 12 o'clock. The family in the morning, when preparing to move to a neighbor's house, not desiring to spend another night in such an unpleasant situation, found some valuable furniture missing. Several citizens occupied the house in their absence as a guard, last night. The same phenomena were repeated; and an attempt to capture the man or thing proved futile, and resulted in the wounding of Mr. James Thomas on the head with a stone.

Several of our informers as these facts were eye-witnesses of what we relate."

The Spirit of Jefferson, Charles Town, West Virginia, December 8, 1868, pg. 2.

ANOTHER MOON GHOST.—The vicinity of Ambler's Mill, in Amherst county, has lately become the scene of the meanderings of a ghost, the appearance of which, shrouded in the vestments of the dead, has frightened to an alarming extent all the timid people of the neighborhood, and has put even the more staid and resolute on the *qui vive*[27] as to who the frightful creature is. His visits are confined, as yet, to the cemeteries in the neighborhood, and it is stated that he warns all who may hear him of the vanity of earthly things, and of the necessity of a preparation for a better world. Somebody, however, suspects that his ghostship is a big, black negro who is operating for his own amusement.—We hope that some brave son of the old Free State will venture upon a discovery of the real facts in the case, and thereby allay the great excitement existing on the subject.—*Lynchburg Republican.*

The Staunton Spectator, Staunton, Virginia, January 5, 1869, pg. 4.

A Ghost—or Something—in Prince William County, Va.

Prince William county is agitated on the subject of a ghost or some other supernatural visitant. A correspondent of the Alexandria *Gazette* tells about is as follows:

For the past few weeks visions of an alarming character have been seen in the neighboring forest, but more particularly in the

---

[27] Latin for being on the alert or on the lookout.

copse adjacent to Mr. Brown's barn and stable. At numbers of times has an immense figure been seen passing to and fro near the barn, with large horns and terrible claws which it contracts to a sort of hoof, and has assaulted Mr. Brown when he attempted after dark to feed his horses and stock, in such a manner, and with such violence, that he has been compelled to flee to his house for safety. The figure, to the best of Mr. Brown's recollection, seems about three times as large as a man in its front, and having a back converging from its neck and shoulders, horizontally to the distance of some six or eight feet, and supplied on each side with large and tremendous arms. It is of pale blueish color when first seen, but upon being initiated by the near approach of any person, becomes a deadly white, and issues from its surface a small volume of smoke, accompanied with a sickening smell. This ghoul or unnatural and horrible animal or demon, has been seen as often as four times near Mr. Brown's stable, and when seen, it has lingered till its deadly effluvia[28] has completely impregnated the surrounding atmosphere. One evening Mr. Brown desiring to have another beside himself see this terrible visitant, induced a courageous gentleman whom I shall call Siger, who happened with his wife to spend the evening at Mr. Brown's to go to the stable to feed his horses. Mr. Siger not believing the story, went without hesitation, when upon entering the stable, he was alarmed by the fall, at or near his feet, with a deep rumbling sound, of a tremendous stone. Mr. Siger, without looking to see whence the rock came, picked the stone up, and it was so hot that he was compelled to drop it; upon looking up he beheld the unearthly monster not over fifty yards from him, and the air became quickly filled and inoculated with brimstone! Not wishing to be thought a coward, he did not mention any thing of this at the house, but upon walking home with his wife the same night, he told her of what happened at the stable, and instantly she became alarmed and was carried home in a state of apparent insensibility.

---

[28] An unpleasant odor.

The neighborhood is in a terrible state of excitement, and stops have been taken to investigate this frightening matter.

The Norfolk Virginian, Norfolk, Virginia, January 30, 1869, pg. 1.

THE HAUNTED HOUSE.—The spectres, noises and mysterious lights that recently appeared in the haunted house in Newtown have disappeared, and now the neighborhood has returned to its usual quiet state. Officers Harrison and Stoakes routed the ghosts last week and they have not returned.

The Richmond Dispatch, Richmond, Virginia, May 26, 1869, pg. 4.

THAT GHOST—A SUCCESSFUL EXORCISM—EFFICACY OF IMPORTED JORDAN WATER—THE GHOST DRIVEN FROM THIS SUBLUNARY SPHERE.—A few days since we published an account of the mysterious appearance of a supernatural visitor at one of our principal hotels. Quite a stir among the hotel-keepers was the consequence, several of them claiming the honor of entertaining the distinguished visitor. As the spirit has been exorcised, so that neither can longer boast any superiority, we do not deem it necessary to designate the hotel. It is sufficient to know that the ghost has been, as is fairly believed, quietly put to rest, and that its wonderings are over.

A prominent government official, who presides over an important bureau in one of the departments, and who is noted for his information upon all subjects, and who has devoted much time to astrologic lore, upon hearing of the presence of this spectral visitant, sent a bottle of water, which he had procured from the river Jordan[29] some years ago, to the young man to whom the ghost most frequently appeared, and directed him to pour a portion of the water in a bowl and to place the bowl upon three hazel[30] sticks laid in the form of a triangle upon a table, and when the ghost appeared to endeavor to sprinkle a quantity of water upon it.

The young man was somewhat loth to meet the shadowy form of his visitor, as it were, by appointment on his part, but a young gentleman friend volunteering to watch with him, he could hardly show a good cause for refusal, and the pair accordingly, Saturday night being pronounced a favorable time for the success of their undertaking, took their station in the room which the spirit seemed to adopt as its own, and waited patiently for its appearance.

Conversation was forbidden and lights were debarred, but the moon shone in solemnly through the window, giving sufficient light to make one another, as they were seated on either side of the table with the bowl between them, just visible.

It was nearly 12 o'clock, and the house was still; even the rats and mice seemed to appreciate that there was something abroad in the midnight air, and the young men began to feel instinctively that the time for their test was at hand. The clock struck 12, and with the first stroke, from a quantity of ladies' clothing hanging in a corner of the room to the back and left of the young men, who were facing the door, the spectre glided—clad, as usual, in its suit of gray.

The young man, the favorite of the spirit, was overcome, and, with mouth and eyes open, sat petrified with fear, but after an instant's surprise his companion dipped his hand into the water, and as the object approached the chair of the first young man, threw some water of Jordan upon it. A few drops fell upon the brow of the

---

[29] The river is sacred in Christianity and Judaism as the site where the ancient Israelites crossed to reach the Promised Land and where Jesus of Nazareth was baptized by John the Baptist.
[30] Hazel wood is used to gain knowledge and wisdom. Hazel wood can also offer magical protection and is used to make wands.

young man at once revived him, and he also commenced to besprinkle the ghost, which neither advanced nor receded, but instead of vanishing, as upon other occasions, commenced to shrink to smaller dimensions, continuing to diminish till no larger than one's hand, and finally died out altogether. Lights were procured, and, singular to state, not a drop of water could be seen upon the floor, although quite a quantity had been thrown upon the apparition. The learned gentleman who directed the exorcism feels confident that the spirit will not again make its appearance.

The Alexandria Gazette, Alexandria, Virginia, October 1, 1870, pg. 2.

The Fredericksburg "ghost" has been captured and turns out to be a female of "wandering mind," who has been restored to her friends, and so ends the great ghost humbug.

The Staunton Spectator, Staunton, Virginia, October 11, 1870, pg. 4.

APPEARANCE OF A GHOST.—The people on the western part of town, near Kenmore,[31] are very much exercised about the appearance of what is supposed to be a ghost in that quarter last Sunday morning between 11 and 12 o'clock. It is said that about that time of day, during the shower of rain, Mr. Mills saw a man crawling on his hands along by the fence dragging his feet after him, as though his legs were paralyzed. He spoke to two ladies standing

---

[31] Kenmore was completed by Fielding Lewis (1725-1781) for his family in 1776. Fielding Lewis' wife, Betty Washington Lewis (1733-1797), was George Washington's sister. During the Civil War, Kenmore was used as a Union hospital.

in the door and asked "What does that mean?" Of course they could not tell, and Mr. Mills said that he would see, and stepped out to the fence, which was but some ten or fifteen feet, by which time the supposed man had passed him some few feet. Mr. Mills got over the fence, and started after the man and asked where he was going. The man straightened up on his feet to full height—which was higher than that of a medium seized man—and said in a distinct tone: "I am going down," and vanished from sight. The figure was dressed in the full uniform of a Federal soldier, which was clean and apparently new, with the blue overcoat coming down to near his feet. Mr. Mills did not see the face of the man, but the two ladies did, and say the face was a bronze with hard features.

The persons who say they saw this are of undoubted veracity, and although they do not believe in ghosts, they are unable to account for this sudden appearance and mysterious disappearance in broad daylight. It has created quite an excitement in that part of town.—*Fredericksburg Ledger*.

VOL. I.—NO. 43.] WASHINGTON, D. C., THURSDAY, NOVEMBER 3, 1870.

The New National Era, Washington, D. C., November 3, 1870, pg. 4.

"BELIEVE IN GHOSTS!"
A Reminiscence of Virginia During the War—A True Story.

Believe in ghosts? Well, no; I can't say I do, and yet something I saw in Virginia, one night, during the war, somewhat staggered me, and I have never exactly known what to think about it. I know, though, that Tom Fairfax would swear to their ghosts, or at least one ghost, to his entire satisfaction on the subject.

Tell it to you? Certainly, I will; and maybe, as you are well versed in ghostly lore, you can explain what it was we saw—not Tom and I alone, but hundreds of boys, for we were several days in the same place, and the whole picket line saw it repeatedly. See if any of your German metaphysical works will explain it. I ask, for it puzzles me.

We were camped on some old field near the edge of a dense wood that was remarkable for the want of undergrowth; you could see way into the thick, cool woods, with nothing but the trunks of the trees to obstruct your vision as far as your sight could reach.

The first night we camped there I was off duty, being ill; we were on the alert, for we knew the enemy were not far off, and were expecting to see them at any moment, and our sentries were thrown out to avoid surprise. I heard the alarm during the night from the pickets, and the stir in the camp, but was too unwell to get up and see about it, as I found the alarm not general, and the next morning laughed heartily at the tale of a ghost having driven in the pickets; but when the thing was repeated the ensuing night, I began to think some one was playing practical jokes—either the men or some one who wanted to pass the line.

On the third night I was able to stand sentry myself, and Tom Fairfax and I requested the Colonel to put us on the road. He did so; and as Tom left me and went on ahead to the outer post, he

"BELIEVE IN GHOSTS!"

A Reminiscence of Virginia During the War—A True Story.

Believe in ghosts? Well, no; I can't say I do, and yet something I saw in Virginia, one night, during the war, somewhat staggered me, and I have never exactly known what to think about it. I know, though, that Tom Fairfax would swear to their ghosts, or at least one ghost, to his entire satisfaction on the subject.

Tell it to you? Certainly, I will; and maybe, as you are well versed in ghostly lore, you can explain what it was we saw—not Tom and I alone, but hundreds of the boys, for we were several days in the same place, and the whole picket line saw it repeatedly. See if any of your German metaphysical works will explain it. I ask, for it puzzles me.

We were camped on some old fields near the edge of a dense wood that was remarkable for the want of undergrowth; you could see way into the thick, cool woods, but the trunks of the trees to obstruct your vision as far as your sight could reach.

The first night we camped there I was off duty, being ill; we were on the alert, for we knew the enemy were not far off, and were expecting to see them at any moment, and our sentries were thrown out to avoid surprise. I heard the alarm during the night from the pickets, and the stir in the camp, but was too unwell to get up and see about it, as I found the alarm was not general, and the next morning laughed heartily at the tale of a ghost having driven in the pickets; but when the thing was repeated the ensuing night, I began to think some one was playing practical jokes—either the men or some one who wanted to pass the line.

laughingly said:

"Well, James, old boy, let's find out what material the ghost is made of it comes tonight."

"All right; I'm with you," I replied. "If he's flesh and blood I'd not like to be in his shoes, for I don't intend he shall make a fool of me."

I forgot to mention that in the distance adjoining the field upon which we were encamped were the ruins of an old time Virginia mansion that had evidently been built in the first settlement of the State. The main road running through the wood led past this house, but it was not on that road that the specter had been seen, but upon a by road leading to an old mill on a rapid and deep, and yet very narrow stream of water.

It was a brilliant starlight night; the moon had sunk to rest, after showing her silver crescent to the admiring gaze of those who loved to look upon nature's beauties; and the light being steady and equal, one could see for a good distance. Fairfax was stationed near enough for me to hear his challenge, should any one come that way. In talking the matter over, we had both arrived at the conclusion that some one was trying to pass the lines, and we were determined to catch him, if possible. As time rolled by and nothing came, I gradually ceased to think of it; and my thoughts reverted to home and loved ones, doubly dear to me, and the form of a dear little blue-eyed darling, who was waiting my return with anxious, prayerful heart, was very palpable to my mind's eye; and so deeply was I absorbed that Tom's challenge of "Who goes there? speak, or I'll fire on you!" fell upon my ear without drawing my attention to it till startled by the report of his gun, and, after a moment's dead silence, a yell so thrilling that it curdled my blood.

Looking down the road I saw running toward me on foot, to whose usual fleetness fear had added lightening speed, Tom Fairfax, the dauntless hero of a hundred hair breadth escapes, and closely following after him glided a singular looking blue light that seemed in the distance to be a column of flame about six feet high.

As Tom reached me he exclaimed, "Great God, James, what is it?" and fell in a dead faint at my feet.

As the thing approached me it took the semblance of a headless man wrapped in a pale flame that flickered in the night air, looking just like little tongues of fire licking the shape. Though startled nearly out of my senses, I waited till it was within five feet of me, and fired my gun right into its breast. The flame waved and opened, spun up a foot or two, and then settled back into the flickering sheet of fire, and the evil thing sped steadily on past me toward the old mansion down the road.

I turned to help Tom, and, as I did so, some of the guard from the main road reached us; for, having heard the report of his gun and his yell, followed by my gun, they had not waited for orders, but hurried to our relief, and they saw the thing as it passed on toward the house. We carried Tom to camp, senseless, and a nice spell of brain fever was the result of his fright; and it would take more reasoning power than I ever heard of any one possessing to make Tom think there are not ghosts.

As Tom reached me he exclaimed, "Great God, James, what is it?" and fell in a dead faint at my feet.

As the thing approached me it took the semblance of a headless man wrapped in a pale blue flame that flickered in the night air, looking just like little tongues of fire licking the shape. Though startled nearly out of my senses, I waited till it was within five feet of me, and fired my gun right into its breast. The flame waved and opened, spun up a foot or two, and then settled back into the flickering sheet of fire, and the evil thing sped steadily on past me toward the old mansion down the road.

I turned to help Tom, and, as I did so, some of the guard from the main road reached us; for, having heard the report of his gun and his yell, followed by my gun, they had not waited for orders, but hurried to our relief, and they saw the thing as it passed on toward the house. We carried Tom to camp, senseless, and a nice spell of brain fever was the result of his fright; and it would take more reasoning power than I ever heard of any one possessing to make Tom think there are not ghosts.

None of the men would stay alone on that post, and a squad was left there for the rest of the night. I fully determined to reach the old mansion and make inquiries about it; but we moved our quarters in a hurry next day, and I never knew the secret of the headless man and that road, or what scene of crime that old mill and the ruined mansion have shared between them.

None of the men would stay alone on that post, and a squad was left there for the rest of the night. I fully determined to reach the old mansion and make inquiries about it; but we moved our quarters in a hurry next day, and I never knew the secret of the headless man and that road, or what scene of crime that old mill and the ruined mansion have shared between them.

The Richmond Dispatch, Richmond, Virginia, November 8, 1870, pg. 2.

"THE MOON GHOST."—The Moon ghost has made his appearance again, and is "turning up Jack" generally on his old playground. We shall keep our readers posted as to his movements.—*Scottsville Register*.

THE VIRGINIAN.

Abingdon, Friday, Nov. 18, 1870.

Southwestern Virginia.

The Haunted Ball-Room.

A number of years ago—perhaps in 1840—the quiet and orderly people of our town and vicinity were startled and bewildered by strange and unaccountable noises in a large frame building in the centre of the place, occupied as a whiskey-shop. It was just such a building as ghosts are supposed to love to inhabit, when the nights are dark and drear, and the storm-fiends are wandering abroad. It was a very large one...

and went through the window almost as rapidly as if they had been shot from a mortar. Next day they had wonderful stories to tell of the fearful things they had seen and heard, of what they said to the ghosts and the ghosts said to them, but they could never after be either coaxed or driven into that part of town after daylight had disappeared. They have both gone to the land of shadows, and carried with them to the tomb an implicit belief in the supernatural.

Two others, who claimed to have more nerve and daring than their predecessors, took their turn the following night, with about the same results, as far as any satisfactory discovery was made. Like the others, they claimed to have seen and talked with the hobgoblins, and to have

their nether garments, and *nothing else!* The other has since informed us that he had often wondered how he refrained from irreverent merriment in the very presence of the dreaded demons of the haunted ball-room, as his companion, with lengthened visage and solemn accents, read the sacred page and uttered his supplications, with nothing upon him but one more garment than Adam wore before he ate the apple and a pair of spectacles!

Their devotions ended, they retired, not to rest, but to await the coming of the mysterious visitants, who thus far had proved the "master of the situation."—True to their habit, as the echo of the last peal of the iron tongue of time in the Court House steeple floated away on

The Abingdon Virginian, Abingdon, Virginia, November 18, 1870, pg. 1.

Southwestern Virginia
The Haunted Ball-Room.

A number of years ago—perhaps in 1840—the quiet and orderly people of our town and vicinity were startled and bewildered by strange and unaccountable noises in a large frame building in the centre of the place, occupied as a whiskey-shop. It was just such a building as ghosts are supposed to love to inhabit, when the nights are dark and drear, and the storm-fiends are wandering abroad. It was a very large one-story building, built expressly for a ball-room, but at the time of the occurrences we are about to relate, the one large room had a bar partitioned off in one corner, and a small bed-room in another corner, the whole ceiled inside with plank instead of laths and plaster. There was no access to the garret save through two stove-pipe holes, and these were too small for even a child to pass through.

One dark and stormy night in mid-summer, after all honest people had retired to rest, the noises of the village were still, and the negroes and their more degraded white companions were sweltering and snoring on the floor of the old ball-room, not only the inmates, but the sleepers in adjacent buildings, were roused from their slumbers by strange and startling sounds. Whilst from one part of the large dark room came deep and suppressed tones of agony, from a third such groans as might be uttered by a strangling giant—not all at once, but alternating—and to lend horror to the unearthly intonations, an occasional shriek floated out upon the murky night air.—Men in wonder gathered in groups, each asking the other for an explanation, whilst others, in larger companies, searched the premises inside and out for a solution of the mysterious clamor.

It is said if you will touch a tree upon which a katydid is singing its nocturnal ditty, its voice will be hushed in an instant. So with the invisible occupants of the ball-room. While search was being made inside, the room was as silent as a charnel-house, but the moment the searchers left it, the hideous uproar recommenced.

This didn't last for a night, or a week, but for months, until rumors, many of them greatly exaggerated, had gone abroad all over the country, and distant journals speculated upon the mysterious manifestations in the haunted ball-room at Abingdon. Night after night, *not alone but in company with others*, have we stood on the outside of the door of that demon-infested room, and seen strong-nerved men turn pale and tremble as the infernal racket rolled on.

At length the disturbance became insufferable, and a number of persons pledged themselves to unravel the riddle, if within the power of mortal men to do it. But, as it was pretty well understood that the ghosts (for there seemed to be legions of them) were not communicative to multitudes, a number of citizens divided off in pairs, and arranged to try it two at a time, occupying the small bed-room partitioned off in one corner, which was furnished with a bed, table, chairs, &c. Accordingly the first adventure fell upon two men with whom we were well acquainted, one of whom, by way, was a brother of the noted Senator Brownlow,[32] and the other a very sedate but superstitious man, who had served an apprenticeship in a building in front of the ball-room, to which the latter formed an L. They repaired to the room soon after nightfall, each armed with a revolver and provided with a pack of cards and a bottle of mountain "bug-juice," and after playing a game or two of poker, and whistling jigs to keep their courage up, they retired to rest, persuading themselves to hope, if not believe, that the mysterious visitants would scarcely dare to hold their accustomed revel in such a presence. But they were mistaken.—About the "witching hour of night," when ghosts most love to wander, and when all was still save the signing night-wind as is chanted its mournful music through the open crevices, they were startled from their troubled slumbers by noises to which, as they described them, bedlam, in its wildest ravings, were as gentle as the breathing of a lute! Their light was burning brightly, and as they sprang from the bed, and looking at each other suspiciously for a moment, as if each supposed the other to be as apparition, standing face to face, dumb-founded and trembling, while the fearful tumult rolled on in the outer room, they were soon brought to a full realization of their surroundings. Without exchanging a word, or attempting to make an investigation of the matter they were there to solve, they each seemed to be moved by the same impulse at the same moment, and went through the window almost as rapidly as if they had been shot from a mortar. Next day they had wonderful stories to tell of the fearful things they

---

[32] William G. Brownlow (1805-1877) was the Governor of Tennessee from 1865 to 1869 and served as the Senator from Tennessee from 1869 to 1875.

had seen and heard, of what they said to the ghosts and the ghosts said to them, but they could never after be either coaxed or driven into that part of town after daylight had disappeared. They have both gone to the land of shadows, and carried with them to the tomb an implicit belief in the supernatural.

Two others, who claimed to have more nerve and daring than their predecessors, took their turn the following night, with about the same results, as far as any satisfactory discovery was made. Like the others, they claimed to have seen and talked with the hobgoblins, and to have driven them from the building, but two or three gentlemen who entered the little bed-room next morning, were persuaded that the driving was the other way, as two pairs of boots and two hats had been left, which were the size of those worn by the men who had scared away the ghost. From every indication, another couple had escaped through the same window about the same speed.

The third night—and there is said to be a charm in that magic number—the adventure was rather more interesting than either of the preceding. The two persons now selected were in middle life, and had long occupied rooms in the front building, in close proximity to that in which the ghosts held their nightly orgies. It was believed they would solve the problem, if it were not really supernatural, and within the scope of mortal men. One of them was tall and as straight as an Indian, possessed of more than ordinary intelligence and dignity, supposed to be a stranger to fear, ridiculed the idea of ghosts and all sorts of superstition, and scouted the notion of a supernatural agency producing a natural manifestation, upon philosophic grounds. The other was not quite so sure that there not such things as ghosts, and consented to the arrangement not entirely without misgivings as to the propriety of doing so, tho' in a common way he was fond of novelty and adventure. It was a dark and drizzly night, the mercury up towards blood heat, and the fitful flows of wind that found ingress thro' the broken window panes, came heated as the breath of a furnace. They entered the room at the hour of ten—just two hours before the usual visits of the apparitions which neither of them were really over-anxious to hear or see, or communicate with in any manner or form. The first was armed with a revolver, a bottle of apple-jack and a bible, and the other with a Presbyterian Confession of Faith, a copy of the National Intelligencer and two North Carolina tallow candles—two thirds cotton and the balance fat.

Neither of them belonged to a church, but before they got out of the building, as the sequel will show, they would have felt more comfortable if they had belonged to all the religious denominations in Christendom and all the auxiliary societies. The night being so excessively warm and oppressive, they divested themselves of outward adornments to an unmentionable extent, and sat down to read and mediate upon the coming midnight, and to train their nerves for the tension to which they might be subjected. The latter had selected the Confession of the Faith and the National Intelligencer, because he had learned that a Coroner's jury had once, upon a time decided that an unknown dead man was both a christian and a gentleman, because the Confession was found in one of his pockets and the Intelligencer in the other. The ghosts, therefore, he thought, if they were as intelligent and considerate as ghosts ought to be, might arrive at the same conclusion with regard to him, and deal gently with him.

The elder and more sedate personage, with a view, we presume, of employing their waiting hours the more profitably, read aloud from the Word, which he had turned down in dog-ears, and instead of dispelling their gloomy thoughts by the soul-stirring songs of Solomon, or the grander inspirations of Isaiah or Jeremiah, chose the sombre stories of the Witch of Endor and the coming together of the dry bones of the valley—themes, as his companion thought, in his then state of mind, not peculiarly appropriate to the place or the occasion.

After reading all such portions as were surcharged with ghosts, hobgoblins and fearful incantations, or as many of them as his memory could conveniently muster, he very reverently closed the volume, and with uplifted eyes and pious emotion, very much surprised his less devout companion by saying "Let us pray!"— They knelt down, and solemn as were the occasion and circumstances, it certainly would have been a scene more ludicrous than sacred to a spectator, had he seen them kneeling amid barrels and bottles of villainous corn whiskey, each attired in their nether garments, and *nothing else!* The other has since informed us that he had often wondered how he refrained from irreverent merriment in the very presence of the dreaded demons of the haunted ball-room, as his companion, with lengthened visage and solemn accents, read the sacred page and uttered his supplications, with nothing upon him but one more garment than Adam wore before he ate the apple and a pair of spectacles!

Their devotions ended, they retired, not to rest, but to await the coming of the mysterious visitants, who thus far had proved the "master of the situation."—True to their habits, as the echo of the last peal of the iron tongue of time in the Court House steeple floated away on the midnight air, the invisible intruders announced their coming by manifestations not less hideous than those which startled the ear of Tom O'Shanter at "auld kirk Alloway."[33] The elder of the pair bounded from the bed as if he had been upon the apex of a volcano, and the other felt as if he would like to crawl into an auger-hole and pull it in after him. The former grasped the lighted candle and boldly stepped out into the large dark room where the ghostly revel was in full blast, the other gallantly bringing up the rear, with feelings about as pleasant as a malefactor may be supposed to enjoy on the way from the prison to the scaffold! The former, however, marched boldly to the centre of the room, and holding the candle

[33] Tam O'Shanter was the hero of Robert Burns (1759-1796) epic poem of the same name. In the poem, Tam O'Shanter, a Scottish farmer, encounters a coven of witches at Alloway Auld Kirk.

above his head with one hand, and lifting the other with his eyes toward the ceiling, exclaimed, in measured and solemn tones—"*In the name of God and high heaven who are you and what do you want?*" That was enough for the ghosts, and enough for the ghost-hunters. In an instant the light was extinguished, and the din that followed was indescribable. The younger and less adventurous of the two finding in the darkness that his friend had left him, he looked towards an open window, and the last he saw of him that night was his *flag of truce streaming out behind* as he leaped through the window, in which performance the other was but an instant behind him. Next morning the tracks of four bare feet were found in the mud beneath the window, and full garments for two hanging upon chairs in the little corner bed-room in the haunted house.

This adventure and failure becoming public, no more hunting in couples was done, and the ghosts were permitted to revel on in unmolested freedom till they grew weary of their occupation. A few months subsequently it leaked out that two or three citizens had fixed up contrivances between the weather-boarding and ceiling, which were operated by strings and wires from the garret, and with a "dumb-bell," chains and a wooden ball at the end of a rope, made the mysterious and unearthly noises which were supposed, even by some intelligent people, to be supernatural.—They had sawed out a hole through the weather-boarding in an upper room of the front building, then in the occupancy of one them, which gave them entrance into the garret above the ball-room which none suspected, all being satisfied that there was no way of getting into that part of the house except through one of the stove-pipe holes, which, as we have already said, were too small to admit even a child. The whole thing was admirably arranged and managed, and completely successful in the accomplishing the purposes for which it was designed.

We have sometimes been charged with knowing more about the ghost than we are willing to tell, as the printing office was in the building in front of the ball-room, but whether we did or not don't effect the story, which is literally true, as, many who heard the noises and narratives of the adventures we have related can testify.

The Staunton Spectator, Staunton, Virginia, December 27, 1870, pg. 1.

A Ghost.

The Lynchburg *Virginian* says that the town of Buchanan, in Botetourt county, has been aroused from its accustomed lethargic state by the pranks of a ghost. It says:

"This Buchanan ghost seems to be of a pious turn of mind, and has taken up his abode at the residence of a preacher, the Rev. Mr. *Thrasher*[34]—a suggestive name which ought to cause this light and ethereal visitor to beware how he cuts his fantastic tricks. But he doesn't seem to mind it, and flies around in the liveliest manner, opening windows, slamming doors, turning things topsy-turvy generally. He doesn't seem to mind bullets, either, else Mr. Walter Johnston must be a shockingly bad shot, and ought to take lessons in target practice. His five balls went whistling in the night air, but no ghost was bagged."

The Alexandria Gazette, Alexandria, Virginia, January 10, 1871, pg. 2.

The Buchanan "Ghost," according to the Fincastle Herald, still continues on the rampage at the house of Rev. George C. Thrasher, despite all efforts to overhaul him. The family of Mr. Thrasher are

---

[34] Revered George C. Thrasher (c. 1823-1873) married Amanda Elizabeth Peck (1834-1901) in 1851.

represented as being seriously troubled by his visits. Perhaps it is the celebrated "Moon Ghost," from Scottsville.

The Evening Star, Washington, D. C., January 13, 1871, pg. 4.

An irreverent Virginia ghost still furnishes an accompaniment of whistling, door slamming and window-rattling whenever Rev. Mr. Thrasher engages in evening prayers. The preacher thinks he would like to justify his name in a personal interview with the impalpable rowdy.

The Alexandria Gazette, Alexandria, Virginia, January 19, 1871, pg. 2.

VIRGINIA NEWS.

The Albemarle ghost appears to have moved to Botetourt county, as already stated. Mr. Moon must be glad to get rid of the ghost and Rev. Mr. Thrasher, no doubt, is inhospitable enough to wish it had never come to his house. The pranks played are similar in both places. No detection as yet.

The Staunton Spectator, Staunton, Virginia, January 24, 1871, pg. 1.

The "Buchanan Ghost"—So-called.

For the past six or seven weeks, occurrences, as yet unaccounted for, have been taking place at the residence of Rev. G. C. Thrasher, a Baptist minister, in Buchanan, Botetourt county, of which the following account is furnished [in] the Richmond *Whig* by a Buchanan correspondent:

"There lives in the suburbs of Buchanan a worthy man, the Rev. G. C. Thrasher, whose house has been for six weeks the theatre if many curious and ghostly exploits. It (whatever it may be) commenced operations by extracting from the reverend gentleman's corncrib, through a padlocked door, a sack of corn and pouring it out some twenty paces from the crib, and this circumstance proves that the spirit must be at least white, for one bearing the hue of the "XVth amendment"[35] could never have resisted the temptation of "toating" it to his haunts. Then night after night it came, performed its fantastic tricks, opened windows barred on the inside, doors locked and guarded, scattered furniture and the utensils of the culinary department hither and thither, and went away unperceived, despite the fact that each night the house was guarded inside and around by vigilant neighbors, armed to the teeth and eager to capture or detect the bold hobgoblin who had time and again passed through their ranks unseen.

One evening last week, whilst Mr. T. was writing in his study, about three o'clock, there was a bold knock on the door several times repeated, but on Mr. T.'s seizing a pistol and rushing to the door, lo! nothing was there and nothing was to be seen in the vicinity, although the minutest search was made; and this knocking occurs frequently, and has been attested by gentlemen of undoubted veracity.

Three evenings ago Mr. T. went over to Dr. Wood's residence, and whilst there heard his little children, whom he had left at home, ringing a bell, and at the same time heard a violent knocking at the door, and on approaching, being armed with a shot gun and accompanied by Dr. Wood, distinctly heard his little son enquire of

---

[35] The Fifteenth Amendment to the United States Constitution was ratified on February 3, 1870, and prohibits the federal government and the states from abridging a citizen's right to vote "on account of race, color, or previous condition of servitude."

the unwelcome visitor what it wanted. A reply was given, but in an undistinguishable mumble, resembling, as Dr. Wood describes it, a confusion of voices coming from the ground. Both gentlemen affirm that not the least trace of any person or thing was visible, although every nook and corner of the premises were carefully examined; nor could any person in the house produce the sounds they heard, no one being at home at the time except his three little children, the eldest a brave little boy of twelve summers, who, with pistol in hand, was interlocuting the hobgoblin who has puzzled the grayest heads in Buchanan.

Some two weeks ago Mr. T. was watching in his yard, armed with a double-barreled shot gun, when, as he says, something like a thin shadow, bearing resemblance to a human form, passed by him, but swiftly as the wind, and instantly disappeared. This is all that he has seen, and strange enough, not a track or trace has ever been left behind, although night after night, in moonshine and darkness, in calm and in storm, the mysterious stranger has come, played his curious pranks, the half of which I have not told, and went—where? One would naturally ask if there might not be some place in which a person might conceal himself for the purpose of playing a joke upon the reverend gentleman; but I answer there is none! Every nook has been examined time and again by many persons; and there cannot possibly be any subterranean retreat for flesh and blood in the vicinity. The surrounding grounds are plain and clear, and it seems impossible that any person could pass from the house unperceived, even in partial darkness."

The Richmond Dispatch, Richmond, Virginia, January 26, 1871, pg. 2.

A RICHMOND GHOST STORY.—*Richmond, Va.*, Jan. 23.— A strange story is told here. Two years ago a gentleman whom I shall call Mr. X., married, and subsequently he became a father. When the child was several months old the mother died. In her dying moments she was exceedingly anxious about her infant and besought her husband to place the child in charge of one of her kinswomen, whom she named. After her death the husband did as his deceased wife had requested, but some time since he married again, and soon reclaimed the child, who could neither crawl nor talk. One day the child was left alone for a few moments in its cradle, some distance from a high bed in the same room. When the second Mrs. X. returned she was surprised beyond measure to find the child lying, smiling and crowing, in the middle of the bed! She asked, in her amazement:

"Who put you there, child?"

And the infant, who had never before spoken a word, plainly replied:

"Mamma!"

The strictest inquiry failed to show that any living person had entered the apartment during the absence of the stepmother. Since then there have been many other mysterious evidences of visitations, spiritual or otherwise, to the child. Whenever the baby was left alone it was heard to laugh and crow, as if it were fondled by some one, but the most sudden entrance failed to catch any one in the room besides the child. A few nights ago Mr. X.'s first wife appeared at the side of his bed, and commanded him to return the child to the care of her relative, as she had directed on her death bed. She threatened, unless this was done, to haunt him incessantly. It is said that the apparition was seen and heard by both Mr. X. and his wife. The result was that the child was carried back next day to the person originally designated by the deceased lady. Such is the tale as 'tis told to me, and that, too, by most respectable and intelligent people.—*Letter in Norfolk Journal.*

The Alexandria Gazette, Alexandria, Virginia, February 1, 1871, pg. 1.

The pranks of the "Buchanan ghost," in Botetourt county, continue, and the mystery is greater than ever. The "ghost" now sometimes talks to Mr. Thrasher's children, but they can never see it. It is Mr. Thrasher's house which the "ghost" visits. Mr. Thrasher says that he has abandoned all hope of solving the mystery, but that he is satisfied by one circumstance that the visitor is a fool. "He said one night that he 'wanted money,' and no one but a fool—be he man or demon—would come to the house of a Baptist preacher for that article."

The Alexandria Gazette, Alexandria, Virginia, February 3, 1871, pg. 2.

The Thrasher ghost in Botetourt still comes and goes; and we see it stated that the Moon ghost in Albemarle has revived. Hardly two ghosts of the same character.

THE PETERSBURG INDEX.

VOLUME X.   PETERSBURG VIRGINIA MONDAY MORNING, FEBRUARY 6, 1871.   NUMBER 156

The Progress-Index, Petersburg, Virginia, February 6, 1871, pg. 2.

The Fincastle ghost has moved out to the residence of a Mr. Curd, a few miles from Fincastle, where he is cutting up all kinds of ghostly capers.

The Richmond Dispatch, Richmond, Virginia, February 7, 1871, pg. 3.

THE MOON GHOST on last Monday night was more rampant than usual. His thumping and rapping on and around the house kept all on the inmates awake. *He*, *she*, or *it*, is no humbug of a ghost. Many of our readers do not believe what has been said of this mysterious affair, but we can assure them that one-half of the mysterious and unaccountable movements of the ghost have not been published. We do not believe that the old detective Hays, reputed to be the best in the United States, could detect the intruder, or account for his being willing to give so much labor night after night, through rain, snow, and mud, in order to annoy the unoffending occupants of the house. It is evident that he is not a thief, for he steals nothing. He had repeated opportunities of stealing Mr. Moon's silverware, but he has never taken anything except a little whiskey and sugar.—*Scottsville Register*.

The Progress-Index, Petersburg, Virginia, February 8, 1871, pg. 1.

The Buchanan Ghost.

A correspondent of the Lexington *Gazette*, writing under the date of Feb. 1st, gives some account of the latest doings of the "Ghost" which has made its appearance at the residence of the Rev. Mr. Thrasher, in Botetourt county. He says:

His Ghostship has entirely changed his tactics again. He rarely knocks at the door now or makes any noise *outside* of the house, is rarely visible, and has for ten days persistently refused either to volunteer to talk or to answer any questions propounded to him. [Perhaps he is offended that your correspondent reported last week scraps of his conversation.] But he has grown still more persistent and violent in disturbing the *inside* of the house, turning the beds topsy-turvy, throwing trash and chips about the house, upsetting barrels of apples in the garret, &c.

We have not space for half of the details but will simply give the occurrences of several days during our stay in Buchanan as we get them from Mr. and Mrs. Thrasher and some of their guests during the meeting of the "Ministers and Deacons' Meeting of the Valley Baptist Association."

On Thursday and Thursday night the disturbances had been actively kept up, and Mrs. Thrasher determined on Friday to use every precaution to stop them, or at least to show that the little girl had no hand in them. Accordingly, after her guests had gone to church she saw her rooms nicely cleaned up, locked each room door, then locked both of the out doors, put all the keys in her pockets, and went into the kitchen with Anna Pring, her little boy and a servant woman, the only persons on the premises, so far at least as was known.

After remaining in the kitchen for an hour or two attending to some domestic matters—during which time no one left the room—Mrs. Thrasher, accompanied by the rest, went into the house again to see if all was right. She found the doors all locked just as she had

THE DAILY INDEX.

WEDNESDAY, FEBRUARY 8, 1871.

The Buchanan Ghost.

A correspondent of the Lexington *Gazette*, writing under date of Feb. 1st, gives some account of the latest doings of the "Ghost" which has made its appearance at the residence of the Rev. Mr. Thrasher, in Botetourt county. He says:

His Ghostship has entirely changed his tactics again. He rarely knocks at the door now or makes any noise *outside* of the house, is rarely visible, and has for ten days persistently refused either to volunteer to talk or to answer any questions propounded to him. [Perhaps he is offended that your correspondent reported last week scraps of his conversation.] But he has grown still more persistent and violent in disturbing the *inside* of the house, turning the beds topsy-turvy, throwing trash and chips about the house, upsetting barrels of apples in the garret, &c.

We have not space for half of the details but will simply give the occurrences of several days during our stay in Buchanan as we get them from Mr. and Mrs. Thrasher and some of their guests during the meeting of the "Ministers and Deacons' Meeting of the Valley Baptist Association."

On Thursday and Thursday night the disturbances had been actively kept up, and Mrs. Thrasher determined on Friday to use every precaution to stop them, or at least to show that the little girl had no hand in them. Accordingly, after her guests had gone to church she saw her rooms nicely cleaned up, locked each room door, then locked both of the out doors, put all the keys in her pockets, and went into the kitchen with Anna Pring, her little boy and a servant woman, the only persons on the premises, so far at least as was known.

After remaining in the kitchen for an hour or two attending to left them, but the beds were all scattered over the floors, and the rooms and passages filled with chips and trash. In one room two logs of wood were crossed in the middle of the floor. This same thing was repeated several times during the day with like results. Friday afternoon, while the family and guests were sitting in the parlor, chips would fly about in a mysterious manner, and no one could be detected in throwing them.

Friday night, Rev. Mr. Whitescarver of Blacksburg, and Deacon Smith of his church were occupying together a room up stairs. Mr. Whitescarver says that before he had succeeded in getting to sleep he saw a man enter the room which at first he took to be Mr. Thrasher. The man walked up to speak, he turned and walked rapidly out of the room, and as he did so Mr. Whitescarver perceived that he was a larger man than Mr. Thrasher and differently dressed. Just as he closed the door after him. Mr. Smith awoke, and he and Mr. W. both distinctly heard him walk heavily down stairs and return as far as the head of the steps. Mr. Thrasher says that he did not leave his room at all during the night, but that he and Mrs. Thrasher distinctly heard the door of their chamber open and shut five or six times in quick succession. This door had been carefully locked when they retired, but was found unlocked the next morning.

The same night, Mr. Dolman—a Deacon in the Jackson Church, Botetourt—was sleeping in an adjoining room when he was awakened by a violent pulling of the coverlids. On jumping up, he could neither see nor hear anything.

Saturday evening, Rev. Mr. Whitescarver felt too unwell to go out to church and was lying on a sofa in the parlor while Mrs. T. and the children were in the dining room—the folding-doors between the rooms being open. Suddenly something heavy was heard to fall in the passage, and Mr. W. went quickly into the dining-room and opened the door leading into the passage. They found a stick of wood lying on the floor, and while talking about it, another fell, until eight or ten large sticks of wood were gathered up. This wood was evidently thrown from the passage above, the stairs go up at this point, but on making the most diligent search no one could be found. Just as they were starting to go up into the garret they heard something fall there, and on unlocking the door and going up they found a large brick in the centre of the floor which had evidently been just thrown there.

Sunday evening violent knocking was heard at the front door; the children reported that they saw a man there who "seemed to vanish through the porch floor," and the knocking then begun violently at the back door. On running there, the children say they saw the same man run off. Mrs. Thrasher now discovered that the back door key was missing, and it had not been found up to Monday morning.[36]

On going back to the rooms they found that the beds had been tousled as usual, and that some pieces of spilt pine (unlike any they had about the place) had been thrown into the rooms and passages.

Your correspondent left on Monday, and has heard nothing since concerning this mysterious affair which, for eleven weeks, has annoyed and baffled this most worthy family.

We have simply "told it as 'twas told us," and will not consume your space with speculations as to the cause of the disturbance. We will only add that Mr. Thrasher says that "he has abandoned all hope of solving the mystery, and is heartily tired of chasing shadows, but that he cordially invites any one to his house who may be disposed to investigate the affair, and will give full possession to any committee who desire to solve it."

---

[36] "By the way, the key which was taken off a week ago, was returned several days afterward," reported *The Progress-Index*, Petersburg, Virginia, on February 15, 1871 (pg. 1).

Staunton Spectator.

VOLUME XLVIII.   STAUNTON, VA., TUESDAY, FEBRUARY 14, 1871.   NUMBER XXI.

The Staunton Spectator, Staunton, Virginia, February 14, 1871, pg. 2.

The Buchanan Ghost.

The unaccountable occurrences which have been taking place at the residence of Rev. Mr. Thrasher at Buchanan for the last twelve weeks still continues, and are still involved in inexplicable mystery. The following is the substance of a portion of a letter written by Mr. Thrasher on yesterday week, as furnished by a correspondent of the Lexington *Gazette*:

"He says that for five days during the week previous the manifestations were frequent, varied and violent. Brickbats, old bones, chips, billets of wood, ears of corn, stones, &c. were thrown about the house in the most mysterious and unaccountable manner, and again and again everything would be turned topsy turvy in the parlor and chambers without their being able to detect the agent.

One day two young ladies being at the house, they determined to use every effort to ferret out the mystery. Accordingly they arranged the parlor, locked all the doors, sent Annie Pring to the kitchen with Mr. Thrasher's little boy to watch her, and carried all the keys to Mr. Thrasher's room. They waited but a few minutes and returned to find that the doors had been opened, the books from the centre table scattered over the floor, the lamps from the mantel-piece put on the floor, and things disarranged generally.[37]

One day Mr. Thrasher himself left the dining room, carefully locked the door and went up stairs to his wife's chamber. Just as he was about to enter he heard a noise down stairs and returned immediately, not having been absent from the room more than *three minutes.*

He found the door open, the furniture disarranged, and all the dishes from the press scattered over the floor. One day the clock was taken from the mantel-piece and put on the floor."

The Richmond Dispatch, Richmond, Virginia, March 4, 1871, pg. 3.

THE BUCHANAN GHOST.—Information which we regard as strictly reliable justifies us in expressing the opinion that the so-called "ghost," which has given the village of Buchanan so much notoriety of late, is a miserable swindle, gotten up by certain interested parties for purposes of their own, and that the alleged tricks of the visitor have been greatly exaggerated. Not to put too fine a point on it, the house at present occupied by Rev. Thrasher is for sale, and somebody who is anxious to buy it for less than its value has concocted these pretended ghostly visitations with the hope of deterring others from bidding from it. We are assured that this is the whole secret of the matter, and that persons in the

---

[37] "And to increase the mystery they found a strange key that would neither unlock or lock any door in the house, sticking in the key-hole of the parlor door," reported *The Progress-Index*, Petersburg, Virginia, on February 15, 1871 (pg. 1).

neighborhood have ceased to pay any attention to the pretended mysterious demonstrations, which have annoyed Mr. Thrasher and his family quite as long as should be permitted, and gained much greater newspaper notoriety than they ever deserved.—*Lynchburg Republican.*

VOL. LXXII.   ALEXANDRIA, VA., SATURDAY EVENING, APRIL 1, 1871.   NUMBER 77.

The Alexandria Gazette, Alexandria, Virginia, April 1, 1871, pg. 2.

The Baptist Church at Buchanan, Va., after an investigation has decided that the "ghost" at Rev. Mr. Thrasher's house, is a "human ghost" and a very mischievous one at that. A girl living in Mr. Thresher's home is supposed to be the ghost, or an aider and abettor of the ghost!

The Alexandria Gazette, Alexandria, Virginia, April 10, 1871, pg. 2.

Rev. George C. Thrasher, at whose house the Buchanan "ghost" has so long carried on his freaks, publishes a letter in the Fincastle Herald, correcting a newspaper statement relative to the probable cause of the manifestations. He avers that the young lady accused with being in collusion with the ghost, could not have known anything about it, and that he is now as much in the dark on the subject as he has ever been.

The Progress-Index, Petersburg, Virginia, April 10, 1871, pg. 3.

THE BUCHANAN GHOST.—We learn that since the recent investigation of this case by the Baptist church, the ghost has entirely ceased his visits, and the whole affair is considered a transparent humbug, which should have been understood by everybody long ago. The only wonder is that it ever deceived even the most credulous; and how those who staked their reputations upon the genuineness of the ghost can now get out of the scrape, remains to be seen.—*Lynchburg Republican.*

The Progress-Index, Petersburg, Virginia, April 18, 1871, pg. 3.

OUR RICHMOND LETTER.
The Hollywood Ghost...
[SPECIAL CORRESPONDENCE DAILY INDEX]

RICHMOND, April 17, '71.

The Hollywood ghost has recently appeared in a new and improved form—in the shape of a woman of great beauty, clothed in lovely raiment, instead of in the old style—old, ugly and dirty. As far as known she was only seen in the Cemetery once—and her visitation on that occasion was noticed by only one or two persons. One of these a gentleman, who lived adjacent to the grounds had the mystery solved next morning when in going to his stable he found a woman lying upon an impromptu bed, which she had made in a corner of straw. He roused her—she gave one swift glance upward and then buried her face under her shawl. The nice appearance of the woman of course excited the curiosity of the gentleman and he plied her with questions, to none of which would she vouchsafe an answer—but at last when the wife of the aforementioned gentleman appeared on the scene she promised to go away provided they would leave her. The gentleman and his wife did leave her—and she immediately came out of the stable and struck a beeline for Hollywood—since that time she has not been seen....

Hollywood Cemetery in Richmond, Virginia. (Image courtesy of Wikipedia).

The Richmond Dispatch, Richmond, Virginia, April 18, 1871, pg. 1.

POLICE COURT, MONDAY—*Justice J. J. White presiding.*— The following cases were disposed of:

...Mary Smith (Hollywood ghost), wandering about the street with no visible means of support. Security required in $100; in default, sent to jail.

Staunton Spectator.

STAUNTON, VA., TUESDAY, MAY 16, 1871.

The Staunton Spectator, Staunton, Virginia, May 16, 1871, pg. 1.

LUCIEN BEARD IN A NEW ROLE.—The Fincastle *Herald* says: We understand from good authority that the horse-thief, Lucien Beard, was the author of the numerous ghostly visitations at the house of Mr. Moon, in Albemarle, which created so much excitement some time ago. In a letter to a friend, the story goes, Beard acknowledged that it was himself who had created the "disturbances," and that he was prompted to do so in revenge for the active part Mr. Moon as counsel, had taken against him when first arraigned on the charge of horse-stealing. Provided with a coat of mail, he was enabled to prowl around with impunity, and the fact that he was not killed by those firing on him, readily created the belief that he was a "ghost." This is a singular story, and should it be confirmed, will doubtless relieve those who were beginning to believe that the seventh vial of wrath[38] is about to be poured out upon us.

---

[38] The seven vials of wrath are a set of plagues mentioned in Revelations 16:1-18. The seventh vial is a global earthquake that will cause all the cities in the world to collapse.

The Alexandria Gazette, Alexandria, Virginia, July 19, 1871, pg. 2.

A "ghost" is raised near the Eagle gold mine in Stafford county. Strange sounds are heard—heard by fifteen persons.

The Daily State Journal, Alexandria, Virginia, July 24, 1871, pg. 1

The Hollywood Ghost—The City Jail to be Haunted.—About 1 o'clock last night, officer Seal of the police found Mary Smith, the Hollywood ghost, lying on the vacant lot just back of the American Hotel. He arrested her and provided her with more comfortable quarters in the second station-house. She was brought before Justice White this morning, who sentenced her to three months in the city jail. Mary will be remembered as having played the part of ghost at Hollywood about a year ago, and also as having been arrested no less than twenty times since on the charge of being a vagrant with no visible means of support. Previous to her appearance at Hollywood, nothing is known of her, as she talks but little, and apparently knows nothing herself of her former life. She is certainly a mysterious character.

The Spirit of Jefferson, Charles Town, West Virginia, October 17, 1871, pg. 3.

—At a colored sociable, held a few nights ago, one of them tried to amuse the party by transforming himself into a ghost. He succeeded well enough to frighten one of the girls into spasms, from the effects of which it is thought, she will not recover.
[*Shenandoah Herald.*]

Virginia's Haunted History

The Alexandria Gazette, Alexandria, Virginia, March 14, 1872, pg. 2.

"THE SMITH CRADLE-ROCKING."—The last number of the Lexington Gazette closes a cleverly written editorial on "Ghosts," with the extract which we give below. The facts of the cradle-rocking are, so far as we are informed, quite correctly given. We have heard the strange story "many times and oft," from the lips of old citizens of Lynchburg:

The Haunted Smith Cradle is now on display at the Lynchburg Museum. (Image courtesy of the Lynchburg Museum, Early Family Rocking Cradle, 2021.27, Gift of Tom Jackson and Joan Coleman).

"This is one of the most remarkable and best authenticated phenomena of its kind on record. It occurred in 1840 in Lynchburg, at the residence of the late W. A. Smith, D. D., for many years President of Randolph Macon College. In that year he was pastor of a Lynchburg church. An empty cradle in his house was noticed rocking of its own accord. It continued its motion for an hour. The next day it commenced rocking at the same time, kept it up, and stopped as on the day before. Thus it continued daily for over a month. Many intelligent citizens and ministers witnessed the wonderful affair and made repeated efforts to solve the mystery without success. It was moved to different parts of the room without any change in its behavior. It was removed to other apartments in the dwelling with the same result. It was taken to pieces and each part scrutinized and refitted, yet there was no change in its motion.

"The Methodist clergy selected one of their number to hold the cradle and prevent, if possible, its movement. The Rev. Dr. Penn, one of the purest men of his time, was chosen for this purpose. While it was rocking he grasped it. It wrenched itself from his grip! He seized it more firmly. The timbers cracked and the cradle would have been broken in the struggle to release itself, had he not loosened his hold.

"It was not further hindered in its daily exercise. After thirty or more days it stopped and never commenced again.

"No explanation of this wonderful affair was ever given or attempted."

The Alexandria Gazette, Alexandria, Virginia, April 6, 1872, pg. 2.

A GHOST STORY.—A letter from Macklenburg county, Va., in the Richmond Whig says:

"I wish to give you now a true story. I conversed on yesterday with a man who has been cured of the terrible disease of epilepsy by a spiritual manifestation. He will be forty-seven years old on the 14th of June next, and has had epileptic spasms constantly since his seventh year. Toward the later part of last August he was taken with one on Wednesday (he does not remember the day of the month), and was too sick to work on Thursday or Friday, and on Friday night he had a horrible dream which awoke him, and on rising up in his bed he saw an old woman, dressed in an antiquarian style, standing by his bedside, who told him that his sufferings had been great and that his yearning prayers for relief had been heard, and he would never suffer again from that malady. He was so much startled that he turned his head, and when he again looked around she had disappeared. He got up at once and examined his doors and windows and found them all fast as he had left them on retiring. He cannot now unravel the mystery. Certain it is, however, that he has not had a recurrence of the spasms since, and is twenty pounds heavier than he ever was in his life, and no fatigue, exposure or excitement hurts him in the least. This statement will of course be read with incredulity, but I know the man personally, and while he is in the humbler walks of life he is a sincere Christian, and I believe perfectly reliable in any statement he makes."

The Raleigh Sentinel, Raleigh, North Carolina, July 17, 1872, pg. 3.

VIRGINIA.

THE McCHESNBY GHOST REDIVIVUS.—On the upper part of Walker's Creek, not far from the scene of the McChesnby ghost, we learn that there have been similar manifestations for the past two weeks at the house formerly occupied by Mr. David Snider. The ghost, or devil, or whatever it is, has taken his old tricks of throwing hot rocks, pancakes, and turning objects generally. The annoyance became so great, as we are informed, that the family have left the house.—*Rockbridge Citizen.*

The Alexandria Gazette, Alexandria, Virginia, October 10, 1872, pg. 3.

A GHOST AT THE JAIL.—For some nights past the guards at the jail have been hearing strange sounds, the cause of which are as yet inexplicable, and the belief is beginning to be entertained among them that some of the persons confined there for murder are to be hung, and that their spirits have commenced to walk the earth already. The sounds resemble those made by rolling at ten pins, and doors, which are shut and mysteriously opened.

The Alexandria Gazette, Alexandria, Virginia, January 4, 1873, pg. 2.

PRINCE WILLIAM ITEMS—
…It is rumored that a ghost of a departed has been seen in this place, causing considerable commotion among some of our people. We have made some inquiries in regard to the matter but cannot get any particulars about its appearance.

The Alexandria Gazette, Alexandria, Virginia, January 21, 1873, pg. 3.

EXCITEMENT.—Some excitement was created on Queen street, between Royal and Pitt, during the early part of last night, by the behavior of a colored man named Butler who lived in that neighborhood and who has lately lost his wife from smallpox. He was running about there in an almost frantic state, uttering shrieks and cries, and swearing that the ghost of his wife had taken possession of his house and driven him away.

The Alexandria Gazette, Alexandria, Virginia, February 21, 1873, pg. 3.

The ghosts whose appearance at the jail was mentioned some time since, have, it is said, recommenced their visitations.

The Alexandria Gazette, Alexandria, Virginia, March 1, 1873, pg. 3.

Ghost or no ghost, it is a hard matter to get a guard who will "stick" at the jail. James Webster, who a few days ago succeeded James Smith, resigned the position yesterday.—Samuel Caton now fills the place, and he says if the ghosts drive him away, no body can stay there.

The Richmond Dispatch, Richmond, Virginia, July 30, 1873, pg. 2.

THE TUNNELTOWN GHOST.—For the last four or five days inhabitants of Tunneltown, in the vicinity of Fairfax and Wilkes streets, have been in the greatest state of excitement. A ghost has appeared to them! Last night, we understand, about one hundred persons assembled to see the spirit, and, if possible, discover the object of its visits, but curiosity as to the latter was not destined to be gratified. The apparition, which is described as a middle-aged white lady dressed in white, glided through the crowd, and though hands were stretched forth to stay its progress, nothing could be felt.—*Alexandria Sentinel.*

The Daily State Journal.

3 CENTS PER COPY.   RICHMOND, VA., TUESDAY EVENING, AUGUST 12, 1873.   VOL. V—NO. 235.

The *Daily State Journal*, Alexandria, Virginia, August 12, 1873, pg. 1.

HOLLYWOOD.—Since the uneasy spirit of Mary Smith was laid to rest in the city jail ghosts do not wander in Hollywood cemetery. Mary is the only authentic ghost of which Hollywood could boast, and even "she now sleeps in the valley," and won't wake any more till Justice White gives the cue.

The *Alexandria Gazette*, Alexandria, Virginia, September 11, 1873, pg. 3.

An old colored man named William Diggs, employed as a watchman at the stables of the street railroad company, has been almost driven by the dread of the ghosts, he swears he sees every night, to relinquish his position.

The *Norfolk Virginian*, Norfolk, Virginia, September 18, 1873, pg. 3.

VIRGINIA NEWS.

Ghosts are reported to be flitting around Alexandria.

The Evening Star, Washington, D. C., January 1, 1874, pg. 4.

SHOT WHILE PLAYING GHOST.—Monday night a youth about sixteen years old, named Michael McDonough, went to the house of a gentleman residing on 17th street, disguised in female attire, for the purpose of playing a prank upon the female occupants. The girls were so much alarmed that it is said one of them fainted, and the others aroused the neighborhood with their screams. W. J. Acree, a young man who was in the house at the time, ran out and fired at McDonough with a pistol, inflicting a flesh wound in the arm. Policeman Ogilvie, hearing the alarm, hastened to the spot, and finding that McDonough had been shot, arrested Acree and carried him to the station house, where he was bailed to answer before Justice White yesterday morning. Young McDonough being unable to appear yesterday, the examination was continued to the 6th of January next, and the accused bailed.—*Richmond, 31st ult.*

The Richmond Dispatch, Richmond, Virginia, January 29, 1874, pg. 3.

Botetourt from Scottsville
...THE MOON GHOST EXPOSED...
[Correspondence of the Richmond Dispatch]

SCOTSVILLE, ALBEMARLE COUNTY, VA.,
January 28, 1874.

Pursuing my peregrinations through Piedmont Virginia, I find myself this evening on the banks of the James where I can stand with one foot on Albemarle soil, the other in Fluvanna, and with a good sling drop a stone in Buckingham's shore....

We have alluded to the Moon ghost, of which the readers of the *Dispatch* a year or two ago will recollect to have seen frequent and startling reports. We visited the locality of these wonderful manifestations a few days since, and not having heard a solution of the mystery we experienced a rather uncomfortable sensation about the head, arising, we presume, from the effort of each individual hair to assume the vertical. Our apprehensions, however, were allayed by meeting a gentleman evidently made after the same image as our self, who informed us that the ghost had been suspected of the very unspiritual pastime of horse-stealing, and being pressed pretty close had taken its flight to more congenial climes. So, our hair resuming the horizontal, we listened to particulars, and gathered, that a band of horse-thieves had been in the habit of visiting the place on their regular trips with their ill-gotten booty, and hid the horses in a dense pine thicket near the dwelling, where they were fed and cared for by a person living on the farm in Mr. Moon's employ, who was connected with the gang. Their reckless characters, doubtless to subserve their own ends, played the strange tricks, which were greatly exaggerated by alarm and frequent repetition. Be that as it may, an arrest or two and criminal prosecution, and the ghost disappeared. Putting this and that together, we confess our belief that the spiritual part of the story has received a severe shock.

The Alexandria Gazette, Alexandria, Virginia, September 9, 1874, pg. 3.

GHOST.—A veritable ghost now haunts that portion of the First Ward known as Tunnel Town. Upon several late occasions, towards the witching hour of night, it has been seen by the fear-oppressed eyes of belated denizens of that locality, as they homeward wended their weary way, engaged in tricks fantastical. It appears in the questionable shape of a beautiful girl, dressed all in white, and of full, voluptuous, but not o'er grown bulk; the phantom whose frolic grace warms the admiration as well as excites the fears of the superstitious beholder, and, when approached by those of younger and bolder blood, who would clutch it and speak to it, flies like a guilty thing upon a fearful summons.

The Norfolk Virginian, Norfolk, Virginia, October 2, 1874, pg. 1.

HAUNTED HOUSE.—We are told that there is a residence on James street which is nightly haunted by the ghosts of a woman and a girl, who make themselves apparently perfectly at home, visiting the different rooms at pleasure, sitting in the chairs, &c., but never interfering with the occupants.

[In this connection, it may be as well to state that our informant is so much inclined to fabricate that we would not advise our readers to put much faith in his ghost stories.]

The Norfolk Virginian, Norfolk, Virginia, October 13, 1874, pg. 1.

GHOST STORY SPOILED.—Some time since the occupants of a dwelling in the western part of the city became impressed with the idea that their house was haunted, and gave it up, moving into another house. He said that locked doors would open and shut without any human agency, and that the steps of a man could be heard at all hours of the night moving restlessly over the house. The son of the owner of the house and another gentleman at last concluded to investigate the mystery, and did so to their entire satisfaction. Before 12 o'clock at night all the noises were made, and proved to be nothing more than unfastened doors and loose window sash.

The Norfolk Virginian, Norfolk, Virginia, January 16, 1876, pg. 4.

A VERY VISIBLE GHOST!—All day yesterday crowds gathered round the residence of Dr. Bilisoly, corner of London and Dinwiddie streets, to witness what was called the ghost of a lady, which appeared at one of the upper story windows. Every newcomer, combining both white and black, were on the tiptoe of expectation, and with palpitating hearts looked up and discovered the terrible apparition. 'Tis the ghost of Miss White, said one, who had died in the house, while another shrugged his shoulders and walked off, exclaiming it was a put-up job. The white-looking bust of a lady was certainly there; thousands can testify to the fact; but as we are not believers in the revisiting of spirits from the other world, we must attribute the figure to some defect in the glass acted on by the sun's rays.

The Alexandria Gazette, Alexandria, Virginia, January 26, 1876, pg. 1.

THE GLASS-GHOST IN PORTSMOUTH.—Crowds from our city continue to visit Portsmouth for the purpose of viewing the "lady and child" in one of the windows of Dr. Bilisoly's residence on High and Dinwiddie streets, and which for some weeks has been the sensation in our sister city. There is no question of doubt as to the representation, and it is worth a visit. People from all sections of the surrounding country, and the strangers arriving on the various steamship and railroad lines, who stop over for any time, are sure to call. At all hours of the day a crowd is present. In company with other members of the press, we made our call yesterday and viewed the spectacle. It represents the head and bust of a female, with a child resting on her shoulder. Her features are distinct, perfect, and somewhat beautiful, reminding one of faces seen in court pictures of the last century, the hair arranged a la pompadour. The features of the child are not so distinct. Through the kind invitation of Dr. Bilisoly, we entered his residence to inspect, and from the inside not a trace of the figure was perceptible, the glass containing the figure appearing the cleanest of all others in the sash.

It was somewhat prismatic in its formation, but otherwise free from all flaw or defect. To the ignorant the "appearance," or "ghost," as it is termed, has caused much wonder, and many amusing incidents are related, one of which is that an old colored woman, a few mornings ago, having on her head a tray containing breakfast for her employer, while looking for the "ghost" saw the little daughter of the doctor come to the window, and supposing her to be the "real ghost" dropped the tray in her fright, and with the exclamation, "Afore God thar it is," and took to her heels. The ferry is reaping a rich harvest, the receipts having greatly increased since the appearance of the sensation.—*Norfolk Virginian.*

The Norfolk Virginian, Norfolk, Virginia, January 27, 1876, pg. 4.

NORFOLK AHEAD.—Norfolk is determined to be ahead of Portsmouth, not by getting up another ghost story, but somebody has discovered a mysterious looking hole away out in the Huntersville road with two sticks stuck on the one side of it, and marks of blood sprinkled around the circular cavity, linking it with perhaps dark and unknown deeds. The mystery seems to be that nobody has observed any human beings at or near the locality to dig up the ground, and it is presumed that supernatural agency must therefore have had something to do with it; or, perhaps the Portsmouth ghost having been so much worried of late by the incessant prying eyes of spectators that it is now solicitous of consigning itself (body and soul) to the quiet neighborhood of the Huntersville road, and so dug its own grave! "Alas, poor ghost!" A certain wag of Portsmouth, however, denies the right of the spirit world to get any credit for this mystery, and asserts that the grave, or hole, arises from natural causes, and that it is more likely the work of the Administration, who are preparing in advance to bury away all records of the late mal-appropriation of Naval funds, which is now agitating the bosom of Congress.

The Valley Virginian, Staunton, Virginia, January 27, 1876, pg. 1.

Ghosts.

The window-pane at the residence of Dr. Bilisoly, on the corner of High and Dinwiddie streets, which bears a stain very much like the form of a woman with a child in her arms, still continues to attract considerable attention. At one time on Sunday afternoon there was between two and three hundred persons congregated on the corner, speculating as to the probable cause of the phenomena. Among the ignorant and superstitious classes the popular opinion was that the figure was the spirit, or ghost, of some person who had died in this residence. This fallacious story, of course, found few supporters among the white portion of our citizens, but it took among the negroes, and numbers of them could be seen on our street corners excitedly discussing the "ghost" theory—*Norfolk Landmark—Portsmouth Column.*

The Norfolk Virginian, Norfolk, Virginia, February 11, 1876, pg. 1.

THE PORTSMOUTH GHOST ABROAD.—Dr. Barrett who lately sent a sketch of the glass apparition of Dr. Bilisoly's window to the Illustrated Police News of Boston, has just exhibited to us a copy of the paper containing the sketch. It is very good with the exception that the Boston artist has not given the lookers-on a very Virginian cast of countenance, and seems to have ignored the fact that more than half of our population are darkies. There is also an explanation appended which has been copied from the VIRGINIAN of the 25th inst.

The Norfolk Virginian, Norfolk, Virginia, February 12, 1876, pg. 4.

THE GHOST MANIA.—A crowd of ghost inspired Senegambians gathered around the Misses Parkers' residence yesterday, at the corner of Glasgow and Court streets, to view a glass spectre said to be on one of the windows on the Glasgow street side. This time it is the picture of a man, who, perhaps, if we adopt the spiritualistic argument, must be the affinity of the lady in Dr. Bilisoly's residence.

The Evening Star, Washington, D. C., March 27, 1876, pg. 4.

ALEXANDRIA HAS A GHOST—a spectre cavalier, in a gray military coat, who rides through the streets at midnight, on a milk-white steed. A watchman at the depot of the Midland road has

seen the phantom horseman—and perhaps snakes.—[*Char.
Chronicle*.

Part IV

The Gilded Age
1877 - 1899

VOL. LXXVIII.   ALEXANDRIA, VA., SATURDAY, FEBRUARY 17, 1877.   NO. 41.

The Alexandria Gazette, Alexandria, Virginia, February 17, 1877, pg. 3.

APPARITION.—The residents of the upper end of the city have been considerably disturbed of late by reports that the ghost or spirit of a former well known citizen, who has been dead about five years, had revisited his home. It is asserted that the spirit at one time came into the room where the family were seated, and produced such a consternation that all of them ran screaming into the street. It is further reported that the spirit is in the habit of returning each night and reading papers and examining sundry documents in a desk and performing other very business like feats. The alleged spirit is that of a once prominent lawyer of the city.

The Alexandria Gazette, Alexandria, Virginia, July 10, 1877, pg. 4.

GHOSTS IN SOUTH WASHINGTON.—South Washington is enjoying a general sensation. It is a haunted house situated on 4 ½ street, between F and G southwest. Saturday evening the crowd around the place was so great at to require the presence of the whole reserve force of the 1ˢᵗ police precinct to preserve order. Last evening the street in front of the house was filled with a crowd of excited persons of both colors and sexes, all eager to hear the latest reports about the engaging topic. It is said that lights are seen, and drums heard to beat and spoons to rattle, and that the two ghosts, male and female, came to the windows, opened the blinds and bowed. Some declared that the female is the spirit of Mrs. Surratt,[39] who was hung at the arsenal. The house has a very pleasant front yard filled with full grown maples.

The street gas light falling on the white-painted door when seen from the street throws a shadow upon it, much resembling a female figure, and it is thought that this first gave rise to the fabulous story. The family who formerly occupied the house left it, it is said, because of these same spiritual manifestations.—*Washington Nation.*

The Alexandria Gazette, Alexandria, Virginia, August 29, 1877, pg. 4.

SENSATION IN PATRICK—A GHOST.—From the Floyd Reporter we understand that quite a sensation has been created in Patrick by a ghost having put in its appearance, or rather having made itself heard, at the house of Mr. Jack Boyce, some six or eight

---

[39] Mary Surratt (1823-1865) was executed for her involvement with the Lincoln assassination. Her boardinghouse is now a Chinese restaurant.

miles from the C. H. We learn that the principal amusement of his ghostship thus far has been hammering, as though driving nails in the floor, and scratching upon the walls. Numerous and varied are the reports as to its operations, and a great many—sometimes 50 at a time—persons have visited the house to witness its doings; all of whom say they heard the sounds but could see nothing. Upon one occasion a young lady, visiting Mr. J's family, it is stated, having retired to her room was aroused by the ghost, and becoming alarmed, she screamed out, when several went to her assistance. They attempted to take her to another room, but she could not get out of bed, whereupon two stout men attempted to lift her out (the young lady is said to weigh only about 100) but were unable to do so. The third man was then called, and it was found to be impossible even to remove the bedclothes. Such are the stories told of the doings at Mr. Joyce's, and a great many, we learn, believe them, and thus quite a sensation has been created in Patrick.—*Staunton Vindicator*.

The Alexandria Gazette, Alexandria, Virginia, April 12, 1878, pg. 3.

A reported ghost that appears in the shape of a boy, or that is manifested by the tramp of invisible horses, now haunts the vicinity of the tan yard nightly, and tends to keep the residents of that vicinity within doors after nightfall.

The Staunton Spectator, Staunton, Virginia, February 4, 1879, pg. 4.

THE GHOST STORY OF A UNITED STATES SENATOR.— The newspaper story that a Richmond house is haunted suggests a ghost story told me to-day by a distinguished senator.—He says he commenced the practice of law in an obscure village, distant from Washington, and one day left his office and went to an orchard not very distant. While eating an apple he cast his eyes to the sashless upper end window of a deserted house, the only one near, and his attention was attracted by the face of a woman who was approaching the window. Her image grew more distinct as she advanced, and when she reached the window her countenance was distorted, as if she was chocked by someone behind her. Suddenly her head and body were thrust out of the window and withdrawn quickly. He hurried back to the village, got a friend, and with him carefully explored the house. The dust in the upper story of the building showed that no one had been there, perhaps, for years, and his ghost story was never explained. He had not eaten apple dumplings for dinner, and was not in love.—*Col. Wm. Gilman in Washington Correspondence of Dispatch.*

VOL. LVI. RICHMOND, VA., MONDAY MORNING, JULY 21, 1879. NO. 18.

The Richmond Dispatch, Richmond, Virginia, July 21, 1879, pg. 1.

The Belle-Isle[40] ghost has occasioned a great deal of talk among the superstitious persons at that place and those residing near the island. A party from this city went over Friday night to witness the actions of the spirit, which is reported to be quite strange. Its headquarters are in the old grave-yard upon the brow of the hill.

---

[40] Belle Isle is an island in the James River in Richmond, Virginia. During the Civil War, 30,000 Union prisoners of war were housed on Belle Isle. Approximately 1,000 Union soldiers died from disease and neglect. Today, Belle Isle is a city park.

Major Thomas P. Turner, in the foreground, commandant of Belle Isle and
Libby Prison, inspects Belle Isle during the Civil War.
(Image courtesy of Wikipedia).

The Norfolk Virginian, Norfolk, Virginia, July 27, 1879, pg. 1.

A Ghost Story.

Norfolk has a ghost story which is creating some little interest in
the upper portion of the city. A young man avers that he has seen
recently and had several interviews with a girl who has been dead a
number of years. He says he has seen her in various parts of the
house, in which he lives, and that she promises to reveal a secret to
him after her tenth visit. No one else living in the house has ever
seen anything unusual there and everybody affects to give no
credence to the story. They do not altogether like the persistency
with which the young man affirms that he has seen the ghost, and
would prefer him to keep quiet about it. He will tell it, however, and

we think it commendable in him. A man who sees anything interesting or exciting and says nothing about it these dull times is neither a friend to the public nor a good citizen. Ghosts are very interesting things, and pleasant to read about. We hope soon to hear of others and further particulars about the one above referred to.

The Richmond Dispatch, Richmond, Virginia, July 28, 1879, pg. 1.

The Belle-Isle Ghost.—The "Belle-Isle ghost" continues to create a great deal of excitement among the people residing on the island and near by in this city. Friday night more than one hundred persons went out to see "his ghostship," near the bridge over the race above the bar-mill, and reported the strange noises produced by the spirit to resemble the splashing of water. Judging from the number of stones, &c., thrown in the race in the direction of the strange noise the ghost will soon move off, or the race will soon be filled up.

The Richmond Dispatch, Richmond, Virginia, August 23, 1879, pg. 1.

The Belle Isle ghost has disappeared, and the excitement it once occasioned has died out.

The Alexandria Gazette, Alexandria, Virginia, August 23, 1881, pg. 3.

A VINEGAR HILL GHOST STORY.—The residents of Vinegar Hill,[41] are much agitated over an alleged appearance of a ghost in the neighborhood, which is reported to roam the hill at midnight on a pure white horse. Mrs. John Verdon, it is said, went to her window about 12 o'clock Sunday night last, and upon looking out saw a strange looking man, tall, with long hair, standing erect on a white horse. This man, who was bare footed, had around him a bespangled blanket, which sparked with a dazzling brilliance. Mrs. Verdon, when she saw this wonderful sight, screamed, and her little daughter, who came to her rescue, testifies that she saw the ghost ride off. Mrs. Verdon was so frightened by the apparition that she is now seriously ill.

The Staunton Spectator, Staunton, Virginia, February 21, 1882, pg. 1.

For the SPECTATOR.

An Hour with a Confirmed Believer in Ghosts.
MINT SPRING, VA., Feb. 8, 1882.

---

[41] Vinegar Hill is the oldest neighborhood in Charlottesville and throughout its history was an enclave for Irish American and African American residents. Vinegar Hill was razed in 1965.

It was the night of the 30th ult. that your writer, in company with Dr. G— of this village, entered the quiet and dreary apartments of a solitary shoemaker, who has recently moved into this community. The subject of this sketch is a man of a tall, lean stature, whose visage plainly indicates years not far short of three score and ten; and, in fact, all features of his appearance bear witness of a life full of toil, and anxiety. Having reared a large family, and now the proud grandfather of bright and happy children, he has returned from the paternal home of responsibilities and careful watching to seek the enjoyments (if any such there be) around a hermit's fireside. He has fostered the belief, from early childhood, that apparitions in various forms walk our earth, and it has now become his second nature. It is not the result of ignorance, or lack of common sense, that engenders this not, uncommon belief, but probably arises more from a deceptive vision.

The time at which we crossed the threshold of his lovely abode was characterized by a dark and starless sky, an hour when imaginative and illusory minds are prone to discard the rational faculties and follow the alluring lights of the *ignis fatuus*[42] to perish in dangerous regions. A bright, blazing fire, cheered the hearthstone, and humble seats were prepared for our comfort. The Doctor, being an inveterate smoker, had a sufficient supply of the weed to divide with his companion and our host; and the pipes being filled to their utmost capacity, the theme of ghosts was next in order.

"Well, my old friend," says the Doctor, who has been for many years a successful practitioner, "do you really believe there are such things as ghosts or spirits?" Our host quickly responded, "I do." "Now," continued the Doctor, "do you not think that many strange and fanciful images which stand across our pathway in dark and dismal places are gaseous vapors arising from the earth?" "Never," replied the old man. "I remember," said the Doctor, with a suppressed smile upon his countenance, "of being aroused at the

---

[42] The Latin term for Will-o'-the-wisp.

dead hour of night to go to see a very sick patient. My road lay partly along the northern slope of a pine thicket. The night was intensely dark and foreboding no good. A grim, white monster of gigantic size, in shape resembling a dog, appeared in my front. My horse became frightened and whirled to retrace his steps. An elegant cowhide and two large cavalry spurs enabled me, with the greatest difficulty, to urge the animal forward. But in the twinkling of an eye, the object vanished, no more to obstruct my course." "You don't tell me, Doctor," interposed our friend, whose very hairs, at this juncture, seemed to point heavenward.

This exciting narrative aroused our old friend to the highest pitch, and he began with relating a series of startling tales, as follows:

"The neighborhood of Old Providence church, where I have spent the palmier days of my life has been the famous spot of my spectral scenes. Were I to go into details of the numerous images, in a variety of shapes and forms, that have appeared unto me, I am sure it would occupy hours, and cause you to shudder and cling closer to your firesides than ever. Not a great while ago I was employed by a farmer in that vicinity to do some work. Night was at hand before I started for my home. I knew my nearest and most direct way was to pass by Old Providence graveyard. The thoughts of this bore heavily on my mind. My heart beat tremulously and fast. A blacker night never curtained the land, and the wind howled long and fierce through the great and mighty woods, as I drew nearer to the slumberer's home. Heaven bears witness to what a frightful object rose from behind a huge, smoldering tombstone, and hastened to welcome my approach. A moment later, and a human form, without a head, all dabbed in blood, stood before me. The very blood in my veins seemed chilled. I tried to speak, but was dumb. Prostration, like the poisonous asp, stole stealthily upon my frame. I felt that I must soon burst asunder the shackles that seemed to stay my progress and make my escape, or else be the monster's victim and sink to earth on the long travel of a thousand years. In a brief moment summoning all my courage, I tore from my perilous situation with a sudden bound, and made race horse time down the pike, never looking back or taking breath until I was seated by my fire. A short time before this, Doctor, I went on an errand several miles from my house and was detained a while after dark. A star-lit sky somewhat relieved the tedium of darkness on this occasion. I had proceeded about half way, and having crossed a chattering rivulet, was ascending leisurely a gently knoll densely wooded, when an apparition, clad in a white flowing shroud, rose on my right, and apparently floating on vampire wings, approached me at a rapid rate. My senses at this time were fully under my control, and you better bet I heeled it away from there, clearing a pair of draw bars nearly eight feet high that stood in my way, never—no, never—taking time for casting, 'one long and lingering look behind.' Again, I remember, Doctor, of lodging in a time worn cabin hard by to a cluster of pines in to the left of Greenville, near what is locally known as South Bottom. It was a dark blustering night. Tradition has it that long ago a man was murdered in that house. Sometime about midnight I was suddenly awakened by the tread of something heavy upon the floor, and all night long that being walked my room floor, now and then uttering the most indescribable, hideous groans."

Thus our superstitious host continued until the hours grew late, and our departure concluded the ghost stories of the evening.

The spirit of an aged woman, long since laid in the silent tombs, frequents this humble cot, and do not be surprised if perchance you hear, in a succeeding hour, of the precipitous flight of our hero before a spirit, but not of the dead.

THETA.

The Alexandria Gazette, Alexandria, Virginia, April 4, 1882, pg. 1.

A Ghost in Staunton.

Staunton has a sensation in the way of a first-class ghost, who holds his sway at the porter's lodge of the Western Lunatic Asylum.[43] The Vindicator, in its account of the ghost, says:

Western Lunatic Asylum in Staunton, Virginia, circa 1891. (Image courtesy of Dale M. Brumfield, American Grotesk)

"On the 6th of February, Junius Slemeker, the gardener of the asylum, aged 55 years died. He was from Richmond, and his wife, while awaiting her return to that city with her children, remained in the residence they had occupied for several years. She stayed about ten days and then removed to Eastern Virginia. After she left the

---

[43] The Western Lunatic Asylum (Hospital) was opened in Staunton, Virginia in 1828. In 1969, the hospital moved to a large facility and the site was converted to a prison. The Staunton Correctional Center closed in 2003. In 2008, the Western Lunatic Asylum complex was converted into condominiums called The Villages at Staunton.

windows were fastened down and the doors securely locked. About five weeks ago, a day or two after Mrs. Slemeker left, Mr. Jewett, who is the watchman of the porter's lodge on alternate nights, heard about 9:30 p. m., while on duty, a violent pulling of the door of the gardener's room, as if some one on the inside was trying to get out. It was so violent and so long continued that he took they key of the room, which is kept in the watchman's room, went across the carriage way, and, unlocking the door, entered and made a thorough search. He found the windows all securely fastened down, and no living creature in the apartment. He made a similar search of the up-stairs sleeping-room with the same result. After coming out and relocking the door he heard the same demonstrations again, accompanied by the sound of breaking sticks and the clinking of iron.

"Another search still failed to reveal anything. He said nothing of the event, but the next night Mr. Wright, who was on duty as watchman, had the same experience, and on comparing notes, the two watch-men found that the noises had impressed each one alike as to the character of the sounds. The report became general, and a number of persons connected with the asylum and some from town have been to the spot and heard the same unaccounted for noises. A few nights ago, as two gentlemen were going down the main building to satisfy their curiosity, they saw from the arch, midway between the asylum and the lodge, a light in the sleeping-room, but on reaching the lodge were told that the door of the gardener's room was locked, and nobody had been up stairs with or without a light.

"The unexplained noises have created a good deal of curious interest in and out of the asylum, especially from their long continuance after every mode of accounting for them has been closely examined into. The whole building, which is not a large one, has been rigidly searched—cellars and all; the doors and windows are securely fastened, and if they were not there is no loose wood or iron in the rooms with which the noises could be made by a person who had entered. The fact that there have been on the ground in the last five weeks (the duration of the phenomena) on various occasions some thirty different persons, and all have heard the same manifestations at about the same time of the night, bars the explanation of auricular illusion, and has added to the curiosity which may now be said to be at fever heat."

The Staunton Spectator, Staunton, Virginia, April 11, 1882, pg. 3.

THE GHOST AT THE W. L. ASYLUM.—We stated last week that it was unfortunate for the insane inmates of that Institution, that the scene of a ghost story should be laid within the grounds of the Western Lunatic Asylum, and were surprised to find sane persons giving credit to it. It turns out, of course, as every sensible person knew before, that there was ghost there. The noises were created by a convalescent patient, who, no doubt, greatly enjoyed the excitement he created in the minds of the credulous and superstitious.

The Staunton Spectator, Staunton, Virginia, April 18, 1882, pg. 2.

KILLS HIS NIECE FOR A GHOST.—Lewis Joice living near Floyd Courthouse was aroused from his sleep several nights ago by a strange noise which proceeded from beneath his bed. After listening awhile, it is said, he concluded that it was a ghost, and grabbed up an axe which he kept at the head of his bed for protection and with great force hurled it in the direction of the strange noise which he said seemed like something sliding on the floor.

The result was he split open the head of his niece, about ten years old, who had gotten up in her sleep and crawled around the floor, and she died almost instantly. An examination was held and the man released from the charge of murder.

The Alexandria Gazette, Alexandria, Virginia, September 30, 1882, pg. 3.

A GHOST STORY.—Firemen on the Virginia Midland Railway tell wonderful stories of the nightly appearance of a ghost on the track of that road, near Otto river, where a tramp was killed some time ago. His ghostship first appeared on two white horses, but, becoming more bold, of late the spiritual stranger, in the form of a man, has dispensed with the steeds, and has several times, unattended, taken a position on the track, in the attitude of the mad bull, and defied the iron horse. One night last week the fireman of an engine discovered what was supposed to be a man on the track. The engine, which was going at a high rate of speed, struck the man and apparently killed him. The train was stopped and several hands were sent back to see what damage had been done. The body was seen a short distance down the road, but upon the men reaching it, it disappeared. At other times the ghost has appeared in cabs of engines, and after surveying things generally, just stepped out into space.

The Staunton Spectator, Staunton, Virginia, October 9, 1883, pg. 1.

Better than a Ghost Story.
A MOST REMARKABLE OCCURRENCE—WHO CAN
EXPLAIN IT?

A remarkable case occurred with a little daughter of Capt. Wm. L. Pratt's, of King George county, last Monday evening. About 3 o'clock she started to the spring, about two hundred yards from the house, for a bucket of water. When about half way, in passing a peach tree near the path, an indescribable sensation came over her. Her hair felt as though it was standing on end and a heavy pressure on the shoulders almost crushed her to earth. With difficulty she walked to the spring, got her water and started back. Arriving at the same tree something came out of the woods in front of her, crossed the path and disappeared. The object appeared to be moving just above the ground. It was covered with something like an old coat, with the sleeves hanging down, on each side. Its head was covered with short, kinky hair, and seemed to have no face, eyes or feet. Its disappearing in an open space seems to be the mystery, as is the further fact that the weakness and pressure left the little girl as soon as it disappeared. The little girl was very much alarmed at the time, and says while this object was passing she could not have moved out of her tracks or spoken if her life had depended upon it. The mother reports that she was as pale as a corpse when she reached the house. Her father Captain Pratt,

Better than a Ghost Story.

A MOST REMARKABLE OCCURRENCE—WHO CAN EXPLAIN IT?

A remarkable case occurred with a little daughter of Capt. Wm. L. Pratt's, of King George county, last Monday evening. About 3 o'clock she started to the spring, about two hundred yards from the house, for a bucket of water. When about half way, in passing a peach tree near the path, an indescribable sensation came over her. Her hair felt as though it was standing on end and a heavy pressure on the shoulders almost crushed her to the earth. With difficulty she walked to the spring, got her water and started back. Arriving at the same tree something came out of the woods in front of her, crossed the path and disappeared. The object appeared to be moving just above the ground. It was covered with something like an old coat, with the sleeves hanging down, on each side. Its head was covered with short, kinky hair, and seemed to have no face, eyes or feet. Its disappearing in an open space seems to be the mystery, as is the further fact that the weakness and pressure left the little girl as soon as it disappeared. The little girl was very much alarmed at the time, and says while this object was passing she could not have moved out of her tracks or spoken if her life had depended upon it.

was in town, and she feared it was a token of some accident that had or would happen to him. She watched steadily for him until he got in sight of the house on his return, when she clapped her hands for joy, and shouted, "Papa is coming." Captain Pratt says he is not a believer in ghosts or supernatural things, but this is a mystery which he cannot explain and which is giving him much concern. The little girl is about eleven years old.—*Fredericksburg Standard, Sept 21ˢᵗ*.

The Alexandria Gazette, Alexandria, Virginia, July 29, 1884, pg. 2.

FACE TO FACE WITH A GHOST.—A telegram from Barbourville, W. Va., of the 27ᵗʰ instant, says: There is great excitement among the mountaineers living in the eastern part of Wayne county over the alleged appearance of the ghost of Harvey Fairman, a farmer, who mysteriously disappeared in 1879. Fairman was supposed to have been murdered, but as no trace of crime was ever discovered, the matter was gradually forgotten. Several days ago Alexander Moore a well-known and intelligent young man was out hunting, and had a curious experience. When at the head of a dark ravine, he says, he was suddenly confronted by what seemed to be a goose or other large white bird, which attracted his attention and then ran into some bushes. Following it, he was startled by seeing before him the ghost of Harvey Fairman, his clothes torn and muddy, and his throat cut from ear to ear. In the conventional hollow tones the spirit told Moore he had been murdered and the body hid beneath the floor of his house for two days, and then brought to the ravine and concealed in a hollow tree. Moore returned home with every appearance of one suffering from extreme terror, and says he will make affidavit to the facts if necessary.

Alexandria Gazette?

VOL. LXXXV.　　　ALEXANDRIA, VA., TUESDAY EVENING. SEPTEMBER 23, 1884.　　　NO. 226.

The Alexandria Gazette, Alexandria, Virginia, September 23, 1884, pg. 3.

GHOST STORY.—The "Editor's Drawer" of *Harper's Magazine* for October contains the following:

"Every one about Alexandria, Virginia, before the late war, knew Captain Charley P—, and many knew him to their sorrow, for he was an inveterate joker (says a correspondent). Poor fellow! I saw the notice of his death in Memphis in the papers last week, and that made me think of what I am going to write. During the war he was clerk for Captain W—, who was depot quartermaster, in charge of the coffins, in the city of Richmond, for the Confederate government. The office was in the rear of a store-house, and the front of the house was filled with coffins. One warm Sunday morning in summer Captain P— thought that he would take a wash and put on a change of clothing. The office being very warm, he thought he would take a nap, and proceeded to look for a good place. He decided at last that a nice clean coffin would be the best then at hand: so he got into one, and went to sleep. He was awakened after a while by a knocking at the front door. He called out, 'Come in.' The door was opened, and a head thrust in, and he heard a voice saying, 'Nobody in.' The Captain had his coat off, and his hair and whiskers were snow-white. Placing a hand on each side of the coffin, he raised himself to a sitting position, exclaiming, as he did so, 'Ha!' The door was slammed to hurriedly, and he ran to it as fast as he could, and, on looking out, saw a countryman dashing up the street as fast as he could, but no standing upon the order of his going. He was rushing over everything in his path, and people thought he was mad. He was evidently seen a ghost."—*Harper's Magazine.*

137

Michelle L. Hamilton

THE NORFOLK LANDMARK.

VOL. XXIII.—NO 117   NORFOLK, VA WEDNESDAY MORNING, FEBRUARY 18, 1885.   PRICE TWO CENTS

The Norfolk Landmark, Norfolk, Virginia, February 18, 1885, pg. 1.

GHOSTS NEAR A BATTLEFIELD.

Strange Scenes Said to have been Witnessed in a House at Rich Mountain.

TEXAS, W. Va., Feb 16.—One of the best known men in Tucker county is Lewis Kittle, who resides in the Indian Fork of Clover Run. His reputation among his neighbors and acquaintances is above reproach, and the following story, for which he vouches, may be relied upon as containing facts as he understands them. Mr. Kittle is not a superstitious man, nor is he a believer in spiritualism. In 1867, Mr. Kittle, in company with others, was engaged in mining near the ground on which was fought the battle of Rich Mountain. He and a cousin named Daniel Courtright boarded at a large house adjacent to the battlefield, and which was used as a hospital for the wounded of both armies. During the progress of the fight one man was shot in one of the rooms, the very room occupied by Kittle and his cousin in 1867. Beginning with their first night in this room, Kittle and his cousin heard strange noises. At first they gave no heed, supposing they were caused by wind. One day they were told by a fellow miner that the house was haunted, and that ghostly forms frequented the room in which they slept. Undismayed Kittle and his cousin continued to remain there.

On a Saturday night soon after this Courtright was absent, and Kittle occupied the room alone. During the night he was awakened by a strange chilliness. A cold grayish mist made the furniture in the room dimly visible. There was an oppressive silence, save for a low, uncertain sound that seemed the echo of a slight breeze.

138

Obeying some impulse, Kittle rose from his bed and moved to a spot opposite and near the door. He felt no fear, but was impressed with a sense of solemnity. Almost immediately he saw in the air eight forms clad in Confederate uniform. With uncovered heads they approached the bed on which Kittle had been sleeping. One of the number removed the bed covering throwing it over the foot of the bed to the floor. Four of the men stooped above the bed as if lifting a weight. The object, wholly invisible to Kittle, was laid apparently upon nothing between the remaining four men, who stood in the position occupied by pall bearers. Two of the men who had lifted the object from the bed took their places in front of the four pallbearers, and two behind them, and in this order the party approached the door. As they passed out, Kittle says he saw lying between the pall bearers the body of a handsome young man, with his coat and vest removed. No sound attended their departure until they reached the hallway, when a noise resembling that made by one walking with a crutch on a wooden floor, followed by the sound of a closing door, was heard.

Kittle returned to his bed, but in almost half an hour the ghostly party returned, performing the same actions as before, except that the body was taken from the floor in the corner of the room. Mr. Kittle says he cannot possibly be mistaken as to what he relates. He was not dreaming, and was wide awake. He was in perfect health. The affair was spoken of at the time to other gentlemen in the house, all of whom agreed that similar experiences had been related by several people who had occupied the room.

On another occasion, and when Mr. Courtright was present, the covering was removed from the bed several times in quick succession. Both men arose and sat on the side of the bed, but were forcibly, though gently, pushed aside and against the wall. They saw no forms near them while being pushed from the bed, but a few moments later saw enacted the same scene described above. Moving the bed made no change in the conduct of the visitors. The visits were so frequent that Kittle and his cousin, on becoming aware of the coming of the soldiers, would say, "There are the rebels."

The Alexandria Gazette, Alexandria, Virginia, July 30, 1885, pg. 3.

THAT PITT STREET "GHOST" AGAIN.—A year or two ago several individuals, at different times, were scared out of a seven-year growth by catching glimpses, after nightfall, of a sombre-clad tall figure, supposed to be of the feminine persuasion, whose wont it was to glide noiselessly along the pavement in front of St. Paul's church, or to suddenly emerge from either of the alleys on that thoroughfare and stand in front of some belated pedestrian until each separate hair on the latter's cranium assumed a perpendicular position. From whence it came or whither it went—hades, the abode of the blessed, Gehenna[44] or sheol[45]—none were able to tell. The spook, or whatever it may have been, rendered many credulous persons nervous, and caused others to go out of their way on more than one occasion rather than risk a sight of the supposed spirit by walking to their homes over the dreaded square. All sorts of suggestions intended to clear up the mystery were advanced, the generally received theory being that the "apparition" was nothing more than a harmless colored woman, slightly demented, who was accustomed to leave her home in the witching hour of night and walk around that neighborhood. The sensation, however, like all mundane things, died out, until last Saturday night, when it once more revived by the "ghost" making its appearance to Mr. James

[44] Gehenna was mentioned in the New Testament of the Bible as the place where children were burned as sacrifices to the Ammonite god Moloch. The valley was located west and south of Jerusalem and takes its name from the Hebrew Ge Hinnom meaning "valley of Hinnom."
[45] Sheol was mentioned in the Old Testament of the Bible as the abode of the dead.

St. Paul's Episcopal Church in Alexandria, Virginia in 1862.
(Image courtesy of Wikipedia)

Wood, who was on his way home at the time. Mr. Wood lives on his way home at the time. Mr. Wood lives on the north side of Wolfe, between Pitt and St. Asaph streets. It was twelve midnight, that lonely hour when grave yards yawn, and lunar's gibbous form had just sunk behind the western hills, when this gentleman, with a box of fried oysters under each arm, started from the Opera House restaurant for his home. He had arrived at the southwest corner of Prince and Pitt streets, intending to pass over the square opposite St. Paul's church, when directly in front of him there suddenly appeared the irrepressible figure he oft had heard of—not in sable habiliments, however, but snowy white. Mr. W. claims to be a disbeliever in ghosts, hobgoblins, fairies or genii, so he determined to catch up with and critically survey whoever or whatever it was that glided—not walked—so stealthily before him. Accordingly he accelerated his gait to the utmost to overtake the spectre, but despite his every exertion he could get no nearer than five feet of the apparition. He smoked up vigorously on a cigar he had in his mouth, for the purpose of shedding as much light on the scene as possible, when, in the twinkling of an eye, the spook vanished as suddenly as a ring of smoke or a burst soap bubble. At this denouncement our hero, sultry as the weather was, felt a cold chill meandering down the spinal column which soon eventuated in a tremor throughout the frame, and concluding that he had had enough of that adventure, became panic-stricken and beat a lively retreat back to the restaurant he had previously left, arriving at which he rushed up to the proprietor in such a disturbed state of mind that the latter imagined him to be in a bellicose humor and prepared himself to act upon the defensive. Mr. Wood, however, soon explained himself by giving a thrilling account of his adventure, which he closed by informing some of the bystanders that they would have to accompany him to his home, as he was completely unnerved. A "committee" kindly volunteered for that purpose, and in the course of half an hour Mr. W. was safe within his own domicile. His disbelief in visitants from the unseen world is not so strong now as formerly.

The Alexandria Gazette, Alexandria, Virginia, January 18, 1886, pg. 3.

A GHOST.—A headless ghost has recently been seen seated on the arch at the intersection of Royal and Wilkes streets. On Friday night last two ladies who were passing that way were so much frightened by the ghost that they dropped a basket they were carrying and ran to the next corner where they told of what they had seen and asked some gentlemen who were standing there to go after their basket, which they did. A man some time ago had his head cut off at that place by being run over by the cars.

The Richmond Dispatch, Richmond, Virginia, August 29, 1886, pg. 4.

A Ghost Mystery Solved and Incendiaries Arrested
[Correspondence of the Richmond Dispatch.]

NORFOLK, August 28, 1886.

...A ghost mystery of several weeks' standing, at No. 42 James street, in which stones and other missiles were projected through the windows and doors by invisible hands at all hours of the day and night was solved last night by the police after a week's watching. A negro boy and his mother were arrested who had been trying to frighten the occupants of the building out of the neighborhood. They were arrested soon after trying to fire the building in two places....

The Alexandria Gazette, Alexandria, Virginia, February 4, 1887, pg. 2.

STONEWALL JACKSON'S GHOST.—A correspondent writes from Lexington the following:

"I send you a thrilling and true account of a ghost which has recently appeared at the Virginia Military Institute. On the night of the 28th, shortly after 12 o'clock, as the sentinel was walking his lonely beat, his attention was attracted through the sally port to the front of the barracks by a slight sound resembling the rustling of leaves by a gentle wind. Instantly, between the two large forty-six pound siege pieces, there appeared a solider dressed in a Confederate uniform and mounted upon a large gray horse. His sword was drawn, his horse tightly reined up, and two white plumes floated gracefully about his hat. The sentinel at first, almost paralyzed with terror, had gazed upon the object, but in an instant, when the horse was started through the sally port into the court-yard at a round trot, crossing the sentinel's beat, making no audible sound, although he was passing over a solid brick pavement, the sentinel, true to his military principle, challenged with a loud voice, "Who goes there?" The rider did not heed the challenge, but passed on at the same pace until arriving at an abrupt, dangerous and impassible precipice in rear of the barracks, he vanished. On the next night a similar phenomena occurred. An old veteran present recognized the grand and imposing form of the rider to be none other than that of Gen. Stonewall Jackson. So far no explanation can be given."

The Norfolk Virginian, Norfolk, Virginia, February 10, 1887, pg. 4.

AGAIN THE GHOST.
Lexington's Pet Sensation—"Stonewall" At Work in His Old Class Room.

James G. Hilton writes from Lexington to the Richmond *State* as follows:

The ghost has ceased to appear until last night, when it again showed itself quite as much surrounded by mystery as on the preceding occasions. At 1 o'clock on the night of February 5th the ghost was seen by the sentinel to emerge from the State library, pass along the first stoop and into class room No. 9. The "officer of the day" and lieutenant of the guard were promptly informed. They forthwith proceeded to Jackson's old class room, where the ghost had been seen to enter. They could see it by the faint light admitted through the window, seated upon the rostrum with book and hat lying on the table in front of it. Its attitude was that a professor listening to a recitation. In a few minutes the figure proceeded to the blackboard, where it went through the maneuver of writing notes on a lecture; then it took from the trough a long pointer in its right hand, faced toward seats usually occupied by the class, and then went through a series of gestures as though delivering a lecture, at intervals placing the pointer on the board as though to explain something written upon it.

After having witnessed the performance for a few minutes, the "officer of the day" and sentinel of the guard entered the room, but no sooner had they crossed the threshold than it vanished. The gas was lighted, and the board thoroughly examined, but no traces of writing could be found upon it. Thorough investigations are being made, and I will advise you immediately if there are any other discoveries. The cadets are trying to keep the matter quiet until an explanation is given.

The Shenandoah Herald, Woodstock, Virginia, February 25, 1887, pg. 2.

Solution of the Ghost Story.

A representative of the *Richmond Whig* the other day questioned a new arrival from Lexington, Va., about the much talked of Stonewall Jackson ghost recently seen in that city. He said for several mornings the life size figure of Gen. Jackson, in full uniform, could be plainly seen upon the front wall of the Presbyterian Church. This created general comment, and for several mornings hundreds of people would come to see the figure, which the superstitious believe verily to be the ghost of Gen. Jackson returning to the church in which he had so often worshipped.

Lexington Presbyterian Church where Confederate General Thomas "Stonewall" Jackson worshipped. (Image courtesy of Wikipedia).

The mystery has at last been solved. Mr. M. Miley, a photographer opposite the church, has a life sized crayon portrait of Jackson in uniform. The rays of the morning sunlight through the skylight struck the portrait at such an angle as to reflect the colors through the window upon the opposite wall. After several days the angle of the light changed, and the supposed ghost disappeared.

The Alexandria Gazette, Alexandria, Virginia, April 18, 1888, pg. 3.

SCARED OUT BY A GHOST.—Though scientific people have urged various theories in explanation of spectres or apparitions, and notwithstanding the belief in ghosts grow less as the years of this century glide by occasionally people of undoubtedly well-balanced minds undergo experiences hard to explain and which serve to increase the credulity of those who believe in the supernatural. Some months ago one of our citizens living on north Washington street, in a fit of despondency placed a pistol to his head and thus ended his earthly career. The family having later vacated the premises, the house was rented by a gentleman from Washington, but the gentleman and his family had not been long in their new home before curious noises, the origin of which it seemed impossible to ascertain, began to be heard, and the belief that the house was haunted soon manifested itself among the inmates. This belief was strengthened about one hundred per cent, night before last by the appearance from the spirit world of the former tenant. The gentleman and his wife, positively affirm that they saw the deceased, and yesterday the family moved out, saying they would not pass another night in the house for the price of.

The Alexandria Gazette, Alexandria, Virginia, May 31, 1889, pg. 3.

SAW A GHOST.—Officers Simpson and Sherwood say that while on duty last night they saw either a ghost or something that looked like what ghosts are said to resemble. They say that while on Franklin street, between Lee and Fairfax, about 2 o'clock, during the storm, and when the night was very dark, their attention was attracted to rustling sounds, and that on looking back they saw a figure clothed in a white, flimsy material, which vanished immediately, the figure ascending into space.

The Times, Richmond, Virginia, July 31, 1891, pg. 4.

THE GHOST STORY AGAIN.
Captain Lipscomb Says That the Old House is Haunted.

I see, said Captain James A. Lipscomb, chief of police, as he cordially grasped a TIMES reporter by the hand, that you are inclined to doubt the ghost story of the old Martin house, an account of which I see in your paper. Well, I just tell you I believe every word of it, and I would not be surprised at anything I heard in connection with that house. Come around to my office and I will tell you a few things. After being comfortably seated in the Captain's cozy office the chief guardian of the city's peace and quiet continued: Though I am not afraid of anything and do not believe in ghosts, yet I would not sleep all night in that old house for a thousand dollars. During the years 1854, '55 and '56 my grandfather, Alexander Reid, Sr., lived in the old Martin house, and all of my leisure moments were spent there. Nothing living or dead, spiritual or human, could have frightened my grandfather but he could not account for the strange noises or sights of that old place. Early one morning the servant girl was sent to the spring for water, but soon came hurrying back frightened nearly to death, saying she could not go, as someone was throwing rocks. The family went out and though they could see the large missiles flying through the air, from whence they came no one could ever tell. It was a nightly occurrence to hear noises such as would be made by the turning over of tables, chairs and the like, and frequently these sounds would come from empty rooms. Strange footsteps, unearthly sounds, &c., were plentiful, but the family had become so used to them that very little attention was paid to them. About a week before the death of my grandfather, I was spending the night with him, when he woke me and asked if I could hear anything. I listened and could plainly hear footsteps and the trailing of what seemed to be a heavy silk skirt. Said my grandfather: twice has a female figure, clad in an elegant white silk gown, come here to my bedside and bending over, looked me in the face. He got up, looked around, but could see no traces of anyone, so, came back to bed. I covered up my head and listened. In a moment or two grandfather jumped out of bed again and this time hurriedly left the room. On his return in a few minutes he lighted a candle and, taking a seat near a small table, began to write. He seemed greatly worried and upon my questioning him said that the white figure again appeared and when he jumped from the bed and made a grasp for it that it hastily left the room through the open door. He pursued it into the lower hall, when it vanished through a closed window. Grandfather only lived about a week after this occurrence and the strange noises became so bad that mother could not wait for the estate to be settled up before she had to move.

Just here the Captain was interrupted by a caller and after a promise that he would tell more of the old house your reporter took his leave. The old house is an old fashioned one, over two hundred years old, and has had the reputation of being haunted for more than a century. It is a wood structure one and a half stories high, with gable roof, situated on a hill in the centre of a pretty grove.

The Richmond Dispatch, Richmond, Virginia, August 1, 1891, pg. 3.

MORE ABOUT THE HAUNTED HOUSE.
Chief Lipscomb Lived There While A Boy

Chief of Police James A. Lipscomb, of Manchester, yesterday, in speaking of the Chesterfield ghost story which appeared in the DISPATCH of yesterday morning, said:

"My grandfather lived in that house when I was a boy, and he once saw the form of a woman pass rapidly down the stairs and glide out of the door in the rear. That night I was sleeping in the bed with him. He turned over, and punching me in the ribs, asked: 'Aleck, did you see that? Did you hear that noise?' Then I heard rattling of dishes and moving of chairs down stairs, but I never did know what made the peculiar noise. My grandfather had never been a believer in ghosts and spirits, but the experience of that night somewhat shook his faith."

In concluding the officer said: "I could tell you a lot about the old Martin house, and I lived there when a boy, and while I am not a believer in haunts, there is certainly something unnatural about that old house."

The Times, Richmond, Virginia, August 2, 1891, pg. 5.

The ghost story recently appearing in these columns has been the cause of considerable talk and revived many scenes and incidents in the lives of the older citizens of our city of by gone spectral visions of white figures and outstretched arms and strange, unearthly sounds.

The American Gazette, Alexandria, Virginia, October 10, 1891, pg. 3.

ALLEGED SPECTRAL MANIFESTATIONS—There is weird talk among railroad engineers and firemen hereabouts regarding the nocturnal appearance on the railroad track near St. Asaph Junction on several nights recently of what is regarded as a ghost, spook, shade or spectre. It is said that on two or three occasions during the night time in the past few weeks, just as a fast passenger train would reach the junction, the form of a man could be seen on the tracks. The supposed human being would be so close to the engine that to stop in time to prevent hitting him was impossible, but upon the train being brought to a standstill no evidence of anyone having been struck could be found. The superstitious among the railroad crews suggest that it is the shade of a man who was killed near that spot several months ago in the night time, and "will not down." The reported apparition has caused some tremor among the nervous in the locality of St. Asaph Junction, and it is said that ramblings around that neighborhood in the "wee small" hours is by no means as common as heretofore.

The Richmond Dispatch, Richmond, Virginia, March 25, 1892, pg. 1.

THE GHOST AT THE COLLEGE.
Captain Hulce Has Detailed a Man to
"Bring in the Spook."

Captain Hulce and one of his faithful's spent an hour and a quarter in the vicinity of Richmond College last night looking for the ghost that is said to have appeared there last Sunday night. Their watching up to the time that the Captain left had disclosed nothing unusual. The mystic figure, or pranking student, was first seen at 9 o'clock on Sunday night by Roger Harrison son of Professor Harrison. He was going diagonally across the field between Grace and Franklin on Harrison street, when he was startled to see approaching him, with a graceful, gliding motion, a marvelous something clad in spotless white.

It came on until it confronted the young man, who was rooted to the spot, and suddenly the terrible object seized the youth. For a moment only it held him. Then it let go and Mr. Harrison took to his heels and did not stop until he reached home. The young man stated that the strange thing looked very much like a woman with a white apron spread over her head. Another gentleman who saw it said that he thought it was a man in his night-shirt.

The general impression is that the ghost is nothing more than a mischievous student or some unfortunate citizen suffering from *mania a potu*.[46]

An officer has been detailed to watch for the unknown phantom, and his instructions are to bring in whatever he may discover to be carousing around in the *role* of a ghost.

The Alexandria Gazette, Alexandria, Virginia, May 19, 1892, pg. 3.

ALLEGED HAUNTED HOUSE.—Some excitement was occasioned on lower Lee street a few evenings since by a crowd of excited women and children who, with distended eyeballs and accelerated pulses, declared a ghost, spook, hobgoblin or something on that order has been seen gliding from room to room in an unoccupied house in that vicinity. A lady, endowed with both nerve and common sense, procured a key and made a reconnaissance and found what is always in "haunted" houses—nothing.

---

[46] Madness caused by excessive alcohol consumption.

The Shenandoah Herald, Woodstock, Virginia, April 7, 1893, pg. 3.

LIBERTY FURNACE REPORT.

MR. EDITOR:—I will give you the following ghost story as told by Uncle Dick, for what it is worth. Late last fall this apparition was seen, mostly in the early part of the night, in the neighborhood of the "old brick yard." All supposed it to be a ghost, it passing around in a generally quiet, easy manner, creating excitement among the women and children. On several occasions some ladies saw it lying on an old log in the day time near what is known as the cold spring. The ladies became very much frightened at the first glance, and not stopping for a second look ran away crying that it was the ghost Uncle Dick saw. Now, Uncle Dick having been a soldier and not of the scary kind, watched its maneuvers very closely, he having the opportunity to do so, and said that to his eye it looked like a man. One night seeing a shadow pass his window he bravely walked out and as he saw it slowly pass away he heard a low, soft voice say very distinctly, "Come down, Uncle Dick." This got to the brave fellow, and he says he wished for a hole in the ground to crawl in and take it in after him. Then he entered the house only to put in a night of fear and horrid dreams. He then came to the conclusion there was something used in the building of a new washer that caused all the trouble. Soon after the washer was moved to a new site and the supposed ghost disappeared. Then Uncle Dick again braved up and said in a boasting way he knew he could foretell the cause of the ghost appearing and disappearing, and many grew wild over Uncle Dick's ghost theory. But a few weeks ago the supposed ghost again made its appearance in the same manner and near the same place, and now Uncle Dick has many callers asking him to explain why the ghost returned. He says he is beat out, but is sure it is not in the washer and also says it takes a man with two eyes to see and tell the strange things that are coming to pass.

The statue *Appomattox* which was removed in June 2020.
(Image courtesy of Wikipedia).

The Alexandria Gazette, Alexandria, Virginia, August 1, 1893, pg. 3.

THAT GHOST AGAIN.—Some years ago it was asserted that a real ghost frequented the square on Pitt, between Duke and Prince streets,[47] and upon several occasions accosted lonely and belated individuals at the weird hour of midnight. It is now said that the ghost has changed its locality and its shadowy form is seem to flit about near the monument at the intersection of Washington and Prince streets. On Saturday night at the same mystic, ghostly hour it reared its aerial form on the gate-post in the moonlight and then disappeared in the trees in the distance.

The Alexandria Gazette, Alexandria, Virginia, October 14, 1893, pg. 1.

A Virginia Ghost Story.

The congregation of a colored Methodist church is much exercised at present over a ghost which is said to have made its appearance in their midst on a recent occasion. One of the deacons of the church a few months ago lost his wife, who had greatly shocked the religionists by her refusal to become one of them. A Sunday or two ago, at night service, the deacon entered the church after the congregation had assembled, and in full view of the people there walked behind him a woman bearing a striking resemblance to his dead wife. The spectators held their breath, watching the gliding figure behind the man, who seemed entirely unconscious of it. He entered his pew with the woman still behind him, seating herself when he did, but presently the stranger was seen to have disappeared, though no one had seen her leave the church by the one door, and the windows were open top and bottom such short distances as to make it impossible for a grown person to have gone

---

[47] The memorial "Appomattox" was erected in 1889 by the United Daughters of the Confederacy (UDC) to commemorate the residents of Alexandria, Virginia that had died fighting for the Confederacy during the Civil War. The statue was removed in June 2020 and given to the UDC which has placed the statue at an undisclosed location.

out at them, even if this feat could have been accomplished without anyone seeing it.

After the service was over all waited to see the deacon leave the church and when he walked away the same woman was discovered walking behind him. The man looked back at the curious crowd, but did not seem to see his companion and when the minister, summoning up his courage, ventured to join him, the figure disappeared.

That night the groans of the deacon roused the other inmates of the house, and going to him he was found to be dying. All were positive that he was alone when they entered the room, which was confirmed by the doctor who was called to attend him, but that as the breath left his body the woman who had walked behind him was seen to leave the room. This is also confirmed by the doctor, who declares himself at a loss to know where she could have come from.

The Old First Presbyterian Church, Alexandria, Virginia, c.1907 (Image courtesy of https://digital.history.pcusa.org/islandora/object/islandora%3A14135/print_object). *The Richmond Dispatch*, Richmond, Virginia, March 29, 1894, pg. 5.

He noticed as she passed him that her garments exhaled a peculiar odor of corruption, and that her face was tied about the jaw after the fashion of arraying the dead. The sister of the dead wife was sitting with the deacon when he died, and, seeing her deceased relative, started up and would have accosted her, but the phantom turned its face to her and went out with a wave of the hand.— *Montgomery Messenger*.

The Alexandria Gazette, Alexandria, Virginia, March 24, 1894, pg. 3.

SAW A GHOST.—While Officers Griffin and Howson were passing the old First Presbyterian Church, on south Fairfax street, at an early hour yesterday morning, Mr. Howson stopped and said he saw something moving about the yard of that church. He approached the iron fence and peering through the bars told his companion that he distinctly saw a shrouded woman moving about the yard. Mr. Griffin closely inspected the premises but says he saw nothing, but Mr. H. persists in saying that he saw the woman. It is stated that a ghost has also been seen recently in and about a house on Royal street, near Prince.

A Costly Ghost Experience.

A few nights ago a young white man undertook to do the ghost act for the purpose of scaring the negroes employed in the blacksmith-shop of the Richmond Locomotive Works. One negro, however, after being frightened nearly to death, summoned up sufficient courage to interview the ghost with a piece of iron. The young man is nursing a severe but not dangerous scalp wound.

Michelle L. Hamilton

The Richmond Locomotive Works in 1911. (Image courtesy of Wikipedia).

The Richmond Dispatch, Richmond, Virginia, October 30, 1894, pg. 1.

SHE SAW THE GHOST.
Was Clad in Black, Had a Sweet Face and Pretty Hand.
THE DISTRUSTFUL CORONER.
He Don't Believe In Spirits Because He Never Saw One—Story of
an Unknown Skull.

At the corner of Fourteenth street and Exchange alley is an old-fashioned two-story brick house, with peaked roof, now divided on the lower floor into two shops, known as Nos. 7 and 9 respectively. According to local tradition its years are considerably over four-score and ten, and though many are the storms that have beaten against it, and though fire has surged around it, the landmark has held its own. Many have been its tenants, and various have been its vicissitudes, and some of its past history—particularly the history of the second floor—is not very savory. The upper rooms have been the den of the "tiger," and those who have not passed middle life can remember when there were dark rumors to the effect that they were supplied with concealed sliding doors and were used as a blackmailing trap. Many a man, it is said, has entered them with a plethoric wallet, and emerged with the aforesaid wallet presenting the appearance of having been trodden upon by the elephant he went to see.

A GHASTLY FIND.

Recently the building has attracted very little notice. No. 9 is used as a barbershop, and No. 7 is rented by Mr. Henry Berkle, a tailor, who, with his family, also occupies the upper floor, and who has been quietly following his trade on the premises for several years. But the structure was only biding its time. Yesterday it again came prominently into notice, to call up spirits, not from the "vastly deep," but from the garret.

It appears that Mr. Berkle had frequently observed upon visiting the garret that some of the flooring was loose, and under it appeared to be a lot of trash. Yesterday, he went up to close one of the windows, and determined to investigate. With the aid of a pole he raked out a lot of rags and paper, then a woman's straw hat with the initials "H. R." marked in it, and finally horror of horrors—

A ghastly grinning human skull was exposed to view.

THE CORONER ARRIVES.

Mr. Berkle notified the police, they in turn notified the Coroner, and that official made all possible haste in reaching the scene. When the Coroner arrived he found that the man or woman to whom the skull belonged was dead, but he wrapped the remains up in a copy of the Charleston (S. C.) Courier, of November 14, 1840, which was found with them, and took them to his office for further investigation.

In the mean time, the story had spread that the house was haunted, and that the inmates had frequently seen a ghost prowling around it. When a Dispatch reporter visited Mr. Berkle's shop last night, that gentleman treated the matter very lightly, and said he had never seen anything "uncanny" about the place.

THE WOMAN IN BLACK.

Not so with Mrs. Berkle. The latter described minutely the arrangements of the rooms upstairs, which she said had a number of doors, and declared that on two occasions she had seen a woman dressed in black, glide through the apartments. The last time the apparition appeared to her was in May. She was not, she said, afraid of it, for the woman had a sweet face and a nice hand.

Mrs. Berkle then went into the backyard, and brought out for inspection three of the "rags" found with the skull. One was a dilapidated bandanna handkerchief, and other a once white silk handkerchief, and a third a coarse apron. All three had spots on them, which Mrs. Berkle said she believed were blood stains. Mr. Berkle said there was a tub full of such rags gotten out of the garret receptacle. Mrs. Berkle is very sincere in her statements.

THE CORONER INCREDULOS.

Coroner Taylor does not believe in ghosts because he never saw one, but that is no sign that there are no such things as ghosts. No well-regulated, self-respecting ghost would interview the Coroner. All ghosts are as skilled as he is in conducting post-mortem proceedings. That is their business. Nevertheless, Dr. Taylor is entitled to his statement. He express the opinion that the skull—no other bones were found—is the "remnant of some doctor or medical student." It bears evidence, he says, of having been prepared in a dissecting-room, and he thinks it was used for the study of the osseous architecture of the head.

Interviews with a number of local historians failed to establish the fact that there had ever been a doctor's office in the building, but, as above stated, its tenants have been numerous.

The residents of the neighborhood of the find are anxious to know whether the skull surmounted the neck of a man or a woman, but Coroner Taylor says that is a question he cannot decide.

The Richmond Dispatch, Richmond, Virginia, November 25, 1894, pg. 1.

THE NORTHERN NECK
A Ghost in the Air in King George County Creates a Sensation.
(Correspondence of the Dispatch.)
COMORN, KING GEORGE COUNTY, VA., November 24....

A FLYING GHOST.

The equilibrium of a quiet section of this county was some evenings ago greatly disturbed by what at first seemed a "sure enough ghost," flying about in the air. The unceasing jingling of chains, etc., overhead broke the silence of the frosty atmosphere from nightfall till the wee small hours, and the bravest men shrank from the awful presence and dared not keep late hours or venture alone from the firesides after dusk. The flying mystery was on every tongue, and no one could doubt the truth of the ghost-story, for the ever-present rattling of chains verified all accounts and baffled all attempts to locate the alarming thing. The consternation it caused and the numberless theories advanced need not be described here. But, happily for the inhabitants of that neighborhood, the mystery has been revealed. A buzzard stepped into a steel-trap, and in struggling to be free broke away the trap, chains, and all, carrying the whole outfit suspended from one foot. Sailing about after dark, finding it impossible to "roost" as usual, the harmless old bird's steel appendages made a peculiar noise, and rendered twilight hideous wherever it went. One well-known gentleman ran himself well-nigh to death, in fleeing from "the ghost in the air," and hysterics was developed in a number of homes.

Michelle L. Hamilton

The Alexandria Gazette, Alexandria, Virginia, January 22, 1895, pg. 3.

Reports from Oxon Hill, on the opposite side of the river, are to the effect that the old mansion is haunted and that ghosts walk through the ancient halls nightly. Strange noises are also heard and the occupants of the house now refuse to sleep there at night.

The Alexandria Gazette, Alexandria, Virginia, February 25, 1895, pg. 3.

The antics of a ghost, or what was taken to be a ghost, attracted considerable attention in the alley running from Duke street between St. Asaph and Washington, last night.

The Alexandria Gazette, Alexandria, Virginia, March 2, 1895, pg. 3.

REAPPEARANCE OF A "GHOST."—About twenty-five years ago some people living on lower Fairfax street positively asserted that occasionally at night a headless man could be seen in that neighborhood. A responsible citizen once averred that he succeeded in getting close to the apparition and that though he could see a collar and necktie on it nothing resembling a head was visible. The ghost, or whatever it was, slinked near a deep gutter and vanished. A year or two later this mysterious visitor again frightened timid people by suddenly crossing their paths at night. The spectre is said to be about again, and last night appeared on lower Fairfax street, between Franklin and Jefferson. Considerable excitement among the superstitious has followed, and some who are not believers in the supernatural are anxious to see the individual.

The Alexandria Gazette, Alexandria, Virginia, March 4, 1895, pg. 3.

"GHOST" CAPTURED.—For several years past what was supposed by the credulous to be a ghost has appeared at night in the neighborhood of St. Paul's Church. At times it was said to resemble a tall women, attired in white. It generally glided from an alley and would vanish before any one could get close enough to make an investigation. A night or two ago it was seen to enter the alley south of the post-office, and on another occasion someone while witnessing its pranks saw it knock at a door on Duke street and when the call was answered by a lady she slammed the door to and ran back in the house. The "ghost" quickly proceeded down the street and was soon out of sight. On Saturday night the "spectre" suddenly appeared on the corner of Duke and St. Asaph streets. A storekeeper in the neighborhood saw the "spook," summoned courage to approach it, and asked what he could do for it. The interrogator received no reply, and deeming he had had enough intercourse with the ethereal visitor left it. Officer Grady arrived on the scene, however, and he not being a believer in the supernatural, called up to the apparition and found it to be a well-known resident of the neighborhood, who, for amusement, was masquerading.

The Staunton Spectator, Staunton, Virginia, May 8, 1895, pg. 3.

A Whistling Ghost.

A correspondent of the *News* reports that there is a whistling ghost at Mt. Solon. If there be ghosts, it is not very strange that there should be whistling ghosts, for that is one of the "fads" of the times. There are whistling women, who make their living by whistling on the stage, notwithstanding the adage that "a whistling woman and a crowing hen never come to any good."

The Richmond Dispatch, Richmond, Virginia, September 8, 1895, pg. 12.

A HEADLESS GHOST.
A THRILLING LEGEND OF SOUTHWEST VIRGINIA.
Johnson's Gorge and Its History—A Story of Treachery and an Encounter with Indians, Ending in a Wedding.
(Written for the Dispatch.)

There are few more weird or solitary looking places to be met with in any part of the country than what is known as Johnson's Gorge. It consists of a narrow gap or pass in the mountains of Scott county, VA., apparently having been cut down by the stream that flows through it, lashing itself into fury as it thunders over its rocky bed and around the jutting cliffs, seemingly in a mad hurry to escape the ghostly gloom that perpetually envelops the place.

On either side the cliffs rise to a great height, and meander in such a way that during the greater part of the year the struggling sunbeams fail to reach the depths of the giant chasm.

About 200 feet up the eastern acclivity is a small plateau about thirty feet square, and, singularly enough, there is a rude natural stairway formed by lodges of rocks, leading up to this plateau, which can be easily ascended by men of steady heads and nimble feet. Back of this plateau is the mouth of a spacious and wonderful cave, which had been explored to the depth of nearly a mile, and which bears unmistakable evidence of having once been the abode of an ingenious and warlike people.

It is little more than a mile from the low, irregular hills that fringe its northern entrance to where the gorge opens out into a beautiful valley, now under a high state of improvement, and embellished with peaceful and happy homes.

A GHOST STORY.

As it is to be expected of a place of such a gloomy and forbidding appearance, Johnson's Gorge has a ghost story—a ghost story of the wildest and most frightful character. Children shudder and creep closer to their mothers' knees at night when the place is mentioned, and many strong men could not be induced to go near the vicinity after nightfall. The ghost is represented as a headless monster of giant proportions, and numerous stories are told of horrible deaths met there in former times by adventurous spirits who "dared the dangerous gloom." Even in the present generation hunters have frequently been driven from the surrounding forests by the fabulous monster.

Ghost stories usually have their origin in some tragic event, superstition working upon the fanciful minds of succeeding generations, and gradually evolving a tale of horror. The ghost of Johnson's Gorge had its origin in an event of treachery and bloodshed enacted there prior to the settlement of the surrounding

A HEADLESS GHOST.

A THRILLING LEGEND OF SOUTH-WEST VIRGINIA.

Johnson's Gorge and Its History—A Story of Treachery and an Encounter with Indians, Ending in a Wedding.

(Written for the Dispatch.)

There are few more weird or solitary-looking places to be met with in any part of the country than what is known as Johnson's Gorge. It consists of a narrow gap or pass in the mountains of Scott county, Va., apparently having been cut down by the stream that flows through it, lashing itself into fury as it thunders over its rocky bed and around the jutting cliffs, seemingly in a mad hurry to escape the ghostly gloom that perpetually envelops the place.

On either side the cliffs rise to a great height, and meander in such a way that during the greater part of the year the struggling sunbeams fail to reach the depths of the giant chasm.

About 20 feet up the eastern acclivity is a small plateau about thirty feet square, and, singularly enough, there is a rude natural stairway formed by ledges of rocks, leading up to this plateau, which can be easily ascended by men of steady heads and nimble feet. Back of this plateau is the mouth of a spacious and wonderful cave, which has been explored to the depth of nearly a mile, and which bears unmistakable evidence of having once been the abode of an ingenious and warlike people.

It is little more than a mile from the low, irregular hills that fringe its northern entrance to where the gorge opens out into a beautiful valley, now under a high state of improvement, and embellished with peaceful and happy homes.

country by the whites. As handed down by tradition, making due allowances for exaggeration, the story is substantially as follows:

From the settlements farther east one balmy morning in early spring a little company of about ten families started forth, carrying their small stores; with them, to seek new homes toward the setting sun. They had heard of the fertile and lovely vales nestled among the mountains farther west, and decided to try their fortunes there, notwithstanding the perils they knew would attend the enterprise.

RICHARD JOHNSON.

Among those hardy pioneers went a youth named Richard Johnson, who was noted for his shrewdness, bravery, and endurance, and who soon became the leading spirit in the adventurous undertaking. Handsome and manly in appearance, with a keen eye that easily rendered him the best shot in the company, and possessing a lively and fun-loving disposition that enabled him to expel the gloom from the ebbing spirits of his friends on the toilsome journey, it is little wonder that the sparkling eyes of the fair portion of the little band grew brighter in his presence.

It was Johnsons invariable custom when the emigrants encamped for the night to make a wide reconnaissance to ascertain whether any foe lurked in the vicinity, for it was as a time when the feelings of the Indians were not altogether favorable to the white intruders, and he was the first to spring to his feet with his trusty rifle in hand upon any unusual sound breaking the stillness of the night. Thus he soon came to be looked upon as the guard of the company, which he, indeed, proved himself to be ere the end of the adventure.

Another character in the company was tall, swarthy, and unprincipled man named David Steers. He was several years the senior of Johnson, and was a thorough scout. He had been among the Indians a great deal, and understood their characteristics much better than any one else in the company. He possessed a wonderful facility for ingratiating himself into the good graces of the red warriors, and went among them with perfect impunity. Of his antecedents the company knew very little. He joined them on the morning of their departure for the West, assuring them of his knowledge of the country through which they were going, and offering them whatever assistance he was capable of rendering. This he at once became quite a hero, and it cannot be denied that his services for a time were very valuable to his companions.

AN UNSCRUPULOUS VILLIAN.

Steers envied Johnson's popularity, but concealed his enmity, openly professing great friendship for the youth. Johnson regarded Steers as a friend, and relied on him as his ablest ally in case of danger. This practically put him in the power of a most consummate and unscrupulous villain. At first Steers simply envied Johnson's popularity, but circumstances soon developed his envy into murderous hatred. Johnson had won the affections of a beautiful girl in the company, named Myrtle Graham, with whom Steers had fallen madly in love, and the latter soon determined to remove the young man from his way.

After a toilsome journey of several days through the unbroken wilderness the emigrants arrived at the valley near the entrance to the gorge, and seriously contemplated locating there, so favorably were they impressed with the surroundings.

Johnson made long explorations of the vicinity, sometimes accompanied by other members of the company, but generally alone. Steers was also quite busy in looking around, and seemed abstracted and gloomy upon his return to the encampment. He had little to say, but his moodiness was attributed to some trivial cause, and very little attention was paid to it.

SIGNS OF INDIANS.

On the second or third day Johnson explored the gloomy gorge, and found that a narrow pathway, well beaten with moccasins, led along the bank of the stream, which had recently been travelled by quite a number of Indians. He also discovered that a white man had been there. In returning from the gorge he observed the rude stairway leading up the acclivity, and saw that it was used by the Indians. These discoveries filled him with alarm, and caused him to hasten back to the camp. After dispatching his supper he was on the point of seeking an interview with Steers, to whom he had decided to make known his discoveries, when, to his surprise, he perceived that individual stealing quietly away into the darkness. Determining to ascertain the intentions of his comrade, he seized his rifle, and stealthily followed him, careful to remain at a proper distance in the rear. Steers started in a direction opposite to the gorge, but made a detour of the camp, and hastened toward the gloomy entrance. On arriving there he paused, and acted in a manner which plainly indicated that he was expecting some one. What could it mean? Johnson crept behind a cluster of bushes, which enabled him to approach within a few feet of Steers without his presence being known, and he soon had every reason to bless the fates that led him thither.

A MASSACRE PLANNED.

Scarcely had he taken his place when he saw several Indians

cautiously approach Steers. He was so near that he could plainly hear every word that was uttered, and what he heard almost froze the blood in his veins. A terrible deed was arranged to be perpetrated, and Steers was to play a prominent part in the fiendish tragedy. The camp was to be massacred, with the exception of the young women, who were to be taken captives. Steers was to have Myrtle Graham as his share of the spoils, and the bloody deed was to be done as soon as the camp had settled down for the night's repose. Steers was to return to the camp and settle down as usual, but was to cooperate with his savage allies upon their arrival in the butchery of his companions'.

Johnson's first impulse was to put a bullet through the traitor's heart, but realizing that that would in all probability only precipitate the intended massacre, he instead made all possible speed back to the camp. His friends must be saved, and the brave boy knew that prompt and effective action was necessary.

The women and children were placed in the rude tent and instructed to remain perfectly quiet. There were about fifteen men and boys in the company capable of handling arms, and as was customary in those heroic times, they were well supplied with "shooting-irons." Each man brought out his rifle and pistols and concealed them under his blanket as the party reclined in various attitudes around the camp-fire. These preparations required but a few seconds. The men were iron-nerved and accustomed to surprise, and the threatened doom was not very appalling to them. In a short time Steers returned, and spreading his blanket, was in the act of lying down when he was pinioned by a pair of strong arms, and in a twinkling bound hand and foot and a gag fixed in his mouth. Johnson then informed him of his doom, and it was with difficulty that he was restrained from hacking off the traitor's head.

TOOK THEIR STATIONS.

Steers was placed near the fire and his blanket thrown over him.

169

Several logs of wood were placed round the fire with blankets over them as decoys, after which the men took their stations a little in the rear to await the appearance of the savages.

Toward midnight a number of dusky forms were seen creeping stealthily from the darkness. When within a few feet of the smoldering fire they uttered a hideous yell and leaped forward, each burying his tomahawk in what he supposed to be a human form. Steers' head was split in twain by a savage blow, and the doom he had planned for his comrades was his own.

At that instant the deadly rifles pealed forth, and seven savages fell pierced with mortal wounds. The remainder thus taken by surprise, fled precipitately, and a storm of pistol shots poured into their retreating ranks brought down three others.

The brave men kept a sharp lookout till morning, but the savages had evidently had enough, and did not reappear.

The emigrants, fearing that the savages would soon return in larger numbers, decided that safety lay in retreat, and at daylight the following morning began to retrace their steps eastward. They reached their old settlement without further incident.

THEY WERE MARRIED.

Tradition says that Johnson and Myrtle Graham were married soon after their return East, and that the following spring they came with a large company and settled in the beautiful valley in which the bloody tragedy was enacted.

Johnson and his fair bride lived to a happy old age, and were unusually prosperous. They left a large posterity to people the surrounding regions.

The gorge, in honor of having saved his friends from a horrible death, was called Johnson's Gorge, and it bears the appellation to the present day.

The above tragedy, Steers' severed head, coupled with a fancied apparition seen by some timid night-walker, no doubt originated the ghost, which is so terrifying to the juvenile portion of the community.

SAMUEL HAYNES.

The Alexandria Gazette, Alexandria, Virginia, September 28, 1895, pg. 4.

GHOST STORY.

More than fifty years ago there stood on the northeast corner of Pitt and Prince streets an old deserted building, which all the children of the town believed to be haunted, and none would pass it at night without fear and bated breath. Near the northwest corner there lived an old colored woman whose ears had been cut for petty larceny and whom the children all believed to be an old witch and they plagued and called her old "croppy" and "witch." The writer in passing loved to plague her by calling her old "croppy" and "witch." She would frequently say "I will fix you." One day near about dark my father told me to go to market and get a beef steak and then call at the shoe maker's and bring home a pair of boots. On his way near the market the writer met old "Phoebe" and commenced to plague her. She replied as usual, I'll fix you. On returning home very dark and thick clouds overspread the heavens and it became very gloomy. When near the corner of H and Prince streets a vivid flash of lightning revealed to him one of the most horrible sights he ever witnessed—a white and headless swan. The writer quickened his pace to the opposite corner when another flash revealed to him this horrible object close to his side. When he arrived home he fell in the doorway as dead. On being revived and being asked what was the matter he stated that a ghost had chased him home. To his dying day he would have believed he saw an actual ghost had not old Phoebe told him a short time before she would fix him. Whatever became of the boots and steak will never be known. The eye of childhood fears the painted devil.

W. J. S.

The Alexandria Almshouse, 1927. (Image courtesy of the Grigg-Lamond Collection, Alexandria Special Collections).

The Alexandria Gazette, Alexandria, Virginia, June 1, 1896, pg. 3.

THOUGHT IT WAS A GHOST.—On Friday night, while the work of tearing up the electric railway track from the Driving Park to this city was in process, Overseer of the Alms House Smith heard the noise, and, supposing some of the prisoners were breaking out, procured his pistol, and, attired in a long night garment made an inspection of the building and found everything secure. He then went out into the lot near where some darkies were engaged in taking up the rails. One of the party got a glimpse of the overseer and, supposing a messenger from Spookland was moving toward him, dropped his crowbar and ran and those who were working with him say he has not been seen since.

The Richmond Planet, Richmond, Virginia, November 21, 1896, pg. 3.

FROM STAUNTON.
A Ghost Scare

Tuesday night, the 10th, one of the neighbors living in Gallos town was disturbed at a late hour by the screams of a certain lady claiming that she had seen a ghost. The neighbors were not able to convince her that it was not a real ghost.

The Alexandria Gazette, Alexandria, Virginia, April 17, 1897, pg. 3.

IS IT CLEM'S GHOST?—There is a rumor among the colored people of the First ward that the spirit of Clem Dorsey, who last week attempted to kill his wife at their home on Gibbon street and then committed suicide by cutting his throat in a neighboring alley, has returned to the earth; that his ghost walks by night and, what is worse, that it carries a razor—presumably for use in case he meets some of those whom he fancied injured him. The story goes that Clem upon reaching the spirit land was so dumbfounded at not finding his wife there that he determined to revisit the glimpses of the moon and ascertain the cause of her stay on earth. To this end it is hinted that Clem's disembodied spirit has been seen hovering around his former abode and that it slowly meanders through the alley where his dead body was found. The thought of a black ghost is of itself sufficiently terrifying, but the idea of meeting one with a gaping wound in its throat and a gleaming razor in its hand is enough to excite the fears of timid people whose business or duty may call them at night to be about in the quiet precincts of the First ward. These rumors may all be incorrect, but certain it is that people whose back yards open upon the alley referred to have observed the quiet that pervades that neighborhood at night, and now back gates can be left open with impunity, and wood piles, coal bins and chicken coops are as safe from marauders as is they were guarded by armed soldiers.

The Alexandria Gazette, Alexandria, Virginia, October 13, 1897, pg. 1.

THE GHOST OF THE BATTLEFIELD.

On that eventful afternoon of the 2d of May, 1863, when Stonewell Jackson hurled his corps upon the right flank of the federal army at Chancellorsville, our battery was attached to the division of A. P. Hill. When we struck the enemy the divisions of Rodes and Colston, which were in the lead, broke their lines before A. P. Hill could deploy, so that we simply followed in the wake of the pursuit in column formation. We proceeded along the plank road for several miles, throwing a few shells now and then at the flying enemy. We then turned off from the road and entered the forest and soon found ourselves in that wild and weird section of country known as the "Wilderness." Night coming on and the battle and pursuit having receded almost out of hearing of us, we began to look around for a suitable place to go into camp. We had been passing the dead and wounded lying upon the ground, as we rapidly followed up the battle, and coming upon one of those small openings that occur here and there in that section, we "parked" our guns and bivouacked for the night. I was sergeant of [the] guard that night and was to go on duty at midnight. The corporal had the first half of the night and came to waken me at 12 o'clock. We had three sentinels, one of whom was over the guns that were "parked" near the skirts of a dense wood. I was sitting in the guard tent trying to read an old newspaper I had picked up on the battlefield by the dim light of a lantern, and had just noted that the time was one o'clock, when I heard the sentinel call sharply, "Sergeant of the guard, post number one!" He repeated his call several times rapidly as I ran towards his post. I found the man with his drawn saber in his hand, pale and seemingly agitated. He said that while walking up and down on his beat as he approached the woods an object resembling a woman clad in white had come out on to the edge of the field and beckoned to him and that it had happened twice before he called out for me. The scene around was lonely and wild enough in all conscience to arose the superstition of most anyone, but this man I knew was one of the staunchest soldiers and I confess I felt somewhat puzzled. I remained talking with him awhile, telling him that he was no doubt mistaken, though instructing him to keep a "sharp lookout," and turned to walk back to he guard tent when my steps were arrested by the sentinel shouting out, "Look, Sergeant, there it is again!" Running back to him, I distinctly saw on the edge of the wood what appeared to be a woman, as well as I could discern in the moonlight, frantically waving her hands and beckoning to us. Seizing the saber out of the sentinel's hand I ran towards the woods with all the speed I could, the sentinel calling after me, "for the Lord's sake" not to go. As I neared the woods the "woman in white" disappeared along what I found to be a narrow path. I followed on the run and had gone about a hundred yards when I pitched headforemost over something lying right across the path. Picking myself up and stooping over to see what it was that had tripped me up I discovered a dead federal solider. I felt on his face. It was cold and he had evidently been dead some time. I could see in the moonlight that the blood had run down and made a dark spot in the sand and his musket was lying by his side. I then walked on a little farther and discovered another, a live on this time and an officer. He seemed badly wounded, his blouse was thrown open and his shirt front was all bloody. He heard my steps and begged piteously for water. "I will bring you some water" I said, and hastening back to camp I awoke the relief, ordered them to get a litter, and catching up a canteen of water returned to the wounded officer and soon had him comfortable in the guard tent. Arousing our surgeon, he dressed the wound and staunched the blood and informed me that had the officer laid on the field another hour he would have died from loss of blood.

We sent him back to the hospital at break of day, and I learned afterward that he was duly exchanged. I reported to the captain what had occurred on my watch. He ordered me to send out a detail to bury the dead solider in the woods, but paid little attention to my account of the woman in white, "saying that the battle had turned all kinds of animals loose in the woods and probably this was a white horse." The sentinel and I did not agree with him however, and to this day all I know is that the appearance of that spectre, or whatever it was, certainly saved that officers life.

J. L. MARYE.

The Richmond Dispatch, Richmond, Virginia, July 24, 1898, pg. 6.

HIS VIEW OF GHOSTS.
CORONER TAYLOR TALKS ABOUT THESE MYSTERIOUS BEINGS.
DOES NOT BELIEVE IN THEM.

The Learned Scientist Not a Supernaturalist, and Says There is No Record of Where an Intelligent Person Has Seen a Ghost.

If there is one man on earth whom ghosts ought to "haunt," and who ought to see "sperits," that one is Dr. W. H. Taylor, of this city.

Everybody knows Dr. Taylor. He is Richmond's wizard, and, besides, there are few pies being cut in Richmond which he hasn't got his finger in, anyhow. First of all, he has that pleasant occupation of being City Coroner. If a body, however harmless and well-meaning, takes a notion to let a locomotive or a street-car run over him and liberate his languishing soul from its prison-house of clay, or if, perchance, he quaffs prussic acid, to the honor of the fair but false one who coldly turns her back upon him, why, it is Dr. Taylor who is the first to be called, and until he has adjusted his steel-rimmed glasses over the remains several times, even the false one, now penitent for what she has done, cannot pillow the fainting head in her lap, or the tender hands of relatives bear away the stiffening form.

IS STAT CHEMIST, ALSO.

Dr. Taylor is also State Chemist, and may expect a brickbat from Albemarle county by most any mail for him to soak in acids and tell what is in it, when every reasonable man knows it is made of nothing but red clay, baked in the Albemarle sun. But the law says the Doctor must "analyze" it—to use a hard word—and send back a long list of things no one would have ever accused the poor brick of being guilty of concealing, only to be read and discredited by the innocent farmer.

He is also a member of the faculty of the Medical College of Virginia, and teaches chemistry and physics in the High School. There he is expected to tell boys and girls that two bodies can't occupy the same space at the same time, and that sulphuretted hydrogen has a delightful odor.

DOES NOT LIKE LAWYERS.

Dr. Taylor is against all lawyers. This he says, is one virtue of his of which he thinks he is pardonably vain. With great complacency he goes on from year to year disliking them as a class most cordial. They have also said some very unkind things about him, and the Doctor would feel badly about it did he not hold to the belief that lawyers seldom say what they think, and only by accident tell the truth.

Dr. Taylor is, moreover, the walking encyclopedia for the city and State at large on all questions of the weird and strange. If there is a shower of meteors or if the moon adorns herself with a ring or whatever turns up or down, for that matter, which is not seen every day in the year, somebody calls up 'Phone No. 692 and asks what he knows about it.

It was quite natural, in view of all this that a scribe of the Dispatch, who wanted to hear something about ghosts, should call upon him for it.

The man whose business it is to inspect dead folks, and who will not even let such harmless creatures rest, one would think would be favored with a perennial visitation of "sperits." But alas, things never turn out as poor mortals expect them.

THE WIZARD IN HIS DEN.

Dr. Taylor was found seated at his desk, in his office on Grace street, only he had wheeled around in his chair and was chatting with a friend when the Dispatch man entered.

"Doctor," explained the scribe, "I want you to give me a real, good, rich ghost experience."

"Why," returned he, "I never saw a ghost in my life, and I never saw a man who could tell the truth who had seen one. I don't believe there is any such thing. Now," he said, "I have heard a lot of ghost stories, and have had my hair stand on end while listening to the tales. I believed them, too, then; but I have outgrown that by this."

When the Doctor reached the point in the foregoing sentence where he alluded to the insurgency of his hair in his youthful days, he put his hand to the top of his pate, yet snatched it away quickly, as if he had lost something and would try to catch it.

DR. LAFFERTY SEES THEM.

"However," the corpse inspector continued, "there is my good friend and Methodist brother, Dr. Lafferty, who believes in ghosts, and has seen many a one. But I tell you, my young friend," mused the Doctor, "don't you believe everything people tell you. Folks are not constitutionally built to tell the truth,, and they don't do it."

"Well, Doctor, didn't you ever see anything at night you couldn't make out?"

"Oh, yes," he replied, "but I stayed there until I did make it out, and didn't run away like I have heard of folks doing who claim they were born to see 'spirits.' If people didn't run, there wouldn't behalf the ghost stories that there are."

Dr. Taylor is too gentle to say so, of course, but he talked along in a strain which seemed to give it as his private opinion that a man who saw ghosts was either very excitable or was careless of the manner in which he handled the truth.

IS NO SUCH THING.

Becoming quite serious, however, the Wizard Doctor said that after all he did not believe in the supernatural. Nature has her fixed laws and conditions, and there was nothing ever seen or ever occurred whose mysterious appearance could not be explained away by them. "I have really given the matter much thought," he declared, "and other men have written books on it, but so far as I know there is not one authentic instance on record where a person of intelligence saw for himself a ghost or a supernatural being.

"Ghost stories usually come down to us via what somebody heard from his grandmother's uncle's aunt's third cousin. At a full meeting of our college faculty one day I asked in all seriousness, because I really wanted to know, if any one present had ever seen or known positively of the appearance of a ghost. All to the last man replied that they had not. The testimony of the leading scientists who have ever lived is that they never saw anything which led them to believe in the transcendental. Among these are Newton, Huxley, Liebig, and others. The only man of science who claims such a thing that I know of is Crookes, the inventor of the Crookes tube, which is used in the X-ray experiments. So you see I could not tell or write you anything about ghosts, though I should try ever so hard, because I never saw one and don't believe I ever will."

The *Alexandria Gazette*, Alexandria, Virginia, August 5, 1898, pg. 3.

THOUGHT IT WAS A GHOST.—Some practical jokers on Wednesday night clothed the fire plug on Christ Church corner on Washington street in white for the purpose of making it look like a ghost. The perpetrators of the joke then secreted themselves for the purpose of witnessing the effect it would produce on certain colored individuals who would pass that way on their return home from an entertainment in the northern part of the city. The parties expected soon afterwards came along, and the antics of some of the belated individuals are said to have been amusing. A number of the party espied the object half a square away and took care to cross to the opposite side of the street. Others came close upon the plug before they noticed it, and went out into the street, passing around the supposed spook and at a convenient distance from it. None, it is said, had sufficient nerve to examine the object, and most of those who saw it had blood-curdling stories to relate when they reached their homes.

The Virginian-Pilot, Norfolk, Virginia, April 1, 1899, pg. 10.

A NORFOLK COUNTY MYSTERY
Farm House Window Haunted by a Ghost.
DROVE A FAMILY AWAY

A Strange Sight Discovered by a Young Farmer, Who, With Many Others Tried in Vain to Solve the Mystery—Man and Wife Desert Their Home—Portsmouth Policemen to the Rescue.

There are mysteries and mysteries, but one has developed in a Norfolk county farm house that bids fair to tax human ingenuity beyond its power to fathom. While it may be divine in its conception it is decidedly ghostly and satanic in appearance, and capable of raising the hair on the head of the average white person, and from the cranium of a majority of the descendants of Cush,[48] the progenitor of the Ethiopian. To state the case plainly and in few words this mystery is a ghost, not, however, of the perambulating species, but stationary and with a partiality for light instead of darkness.

---

[48] According to the Old Testament, Cush was the oldest son of Ham and the grandson of Noah. In the Bible, Cush was identified with Kingdom of Kush, an ancient kingdom in Nubia, now part of southern Sudan and southern Egypt.

A few days ago a young farmer was passing the farm house in question and saw outlined in a large window glass the bust of a woman. Knowing that the house was occupied by negroes he thought it strange that a white woman should be in it, but passed on. Returning just before nightfall, he was still more astonished to find the woman there, glancing toward the road, or rather at him. He brought his horse and buggy to a standstill and proceeded to investigate.

The young man gazed long and intently at the window and thoroughly satisfied himself that the profile was that of a white woman. The hair was smooth and black, the eyebrows heavy and regular, the nose aquiline, and lips thin and regular—all indicative of Caucasian lineage. He left his vehicle, went to the door of the house, knocked and was admitted, and glancing at the window and seeing no one, asked:

"Where is the woman I saw at that window (pointing to it) awhile ago?"

"There was no woman there," answered the colored woman.

"Do you mean to tell me that my eyes deceive me?" he answered, somewhat impatiently. "Didn't I stand out in the road and look straight at her for five minutes? Besides, I saw her there as I passed your house about two hours ago, on my way to Portsmouth."

"Look a here, boss, what you been drinking? There's been no woman here but me. I tells you, and I aint been of'en dis stool by my sick baby's cradle. If it was anybody it mus a been a ghost."

The now indignant and disappointed young man left the house and when about half way to the gate, glanced over his shoulder at the window, and, lo! and behold! the woman had resumed her former station. He called loudly to the colored woman, who soon appeared in the door way. He beckoned her to him, and when she came to his side, said: "Look at that window!"

She took one look and cried:

"Hit's a ghost; I done knowed it. Mr.—, for de good Lawd's sake bring me my baby. I wouldn't go back in dar for six babies, and ise got but one."

THE HOME ABANDONED.

She was frightened terribly, and he, now both mystified and terrified, managed to return to the house and bring out the pickaninny. When the woman, at his command had seated herself in the buggy, he gave her the child, mounted to her side, seized the lines and lashed the horse into a rapid gait. He glanced at the window as the animal started, to find its occupant still looking straight at him. The hair of his head pushed his Derby hat off. He let it remain in the roadway where it found lodgment.

The colored woman could not be persuaded to return to her home. Her husband, on coming in from the field, found only the dog to greet him. The door was open, the cradle empty, the fire out and a feeling of desolation took possession of him. He closed the door, left the house after a long and weary search located his wife and child at the home of the young white farmer, whose name is withheld for prudential reasons.

OTHERS SEE THE WINDOW.

The next morning, accompanied by the negro man, the young farmer drove to the front of the house inhabited by the feminine ghost. A glance at the window revealed her presence. She was in the same position and was apparently there to stay. The negro, who had partially recovered from the fright his wife gave him by her horrible revelation in the early morning, resolved to venture inside. He did so, remained quite awhile, nut finally emerged with the cradle, packed full of things on his shoulder. He called out:

"Nuffin' in dar; you and Maria done gone and got skeered at a shadder [shadow]; but ise gwine to take her dese things, cause she ain't a gwine to come back till I put in a new windah."

"Look behind you!" the young man in the vehicle commanded.

The negro looked, dropped the crib, shrieked "Lawdy, Lawdy," and shot through the gate and down the highway at a speed that would have made Longfellow turn green with envy in his palmiest running days. The young man returned home, where he found the negro, his wife and baby and his mother victims of the terror that possessed them.

The presence of the ghost in the window attracted many visitors to the house. The ghost was impartial and appeared to each, frightening all of ghosts afraid.

THE MYSTERY SOLVED.

Many theories of how the woman succeeded in getting into and becoming a part of the window were advanced. Some said it was an optical illusion, some declared it was a shadow photographed in the process of molding the glass, others vowed that it was a veritable ghost, and still others denounced it as his Satanic Majesty disguised as a woman. The honor of solving the mystery was reserved to Police Officer Adolphus Meginley, of Portsmouth, who, after patient and thorough investigation, reminded both believers and sceptics that to-day was the first of April, and universally known as "All Fool's Day," whereupon the ghost suddenly disappeared and is not likely to be seen in that window again. The colored people returned this morning and the cradle is again rocking to the music of the mothers crooning, the song of the bluebird and the chatter of the English sparrow.

The Virginian-Pilot, Norfolk, Virginia, May 6, 1899, pg. 8.

THE NORFOLK COUNTY GHOST.

Considerably interest was excited here to-day by the mysterious face of a woman which appeared photographed upon a pane in the window of a house at No. 205 West Grace, occupied by Dr. Augus Nichols. It seems to be the face of a young woman wearing a mantilla. Hundreds of people went to see it.

The Times, Richmond, Virginia, July 30, 1899, pg. 6.

THE PASSING OF THE GHOST
His Filmy, Uncanny Presence a Thing of the Past in Richmond.

NOT EVEN A GRAVEYARD SPOOK.
Decadence of the Tribe Dates From the War Which May Have Scared Them Off—New Generation of Darkies Not Superstitions.

Ghosts are going out of fashion. There was a time, not so long ago, either, when spook lore was a most important branch of the literature of this vicinity. Any good old-fashioned black mammy, a few of whom are left as reminders of what many call a happier era, will vouch for the material presence of genuine "haunts," up to the days of the war. The decadence of the ghost tribe may be said to date from the

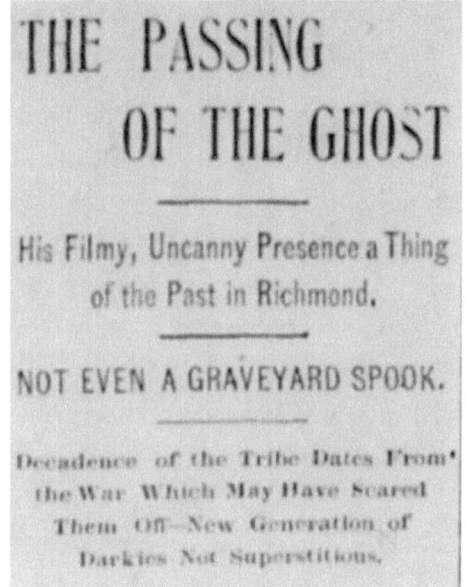

thunders of the big guns throughout the country, and especially in this immediate region. Perhaps the ethereal, sensitive creatures were seated away by the red dogs of war. Who knows? At any rate a ghost is a rare presence now, and The Times is prepared to maintain, after having made a thorough canvas of the community, that there does not exist a real live, awe-inspiring "ha'nt" in the whole of Richmond.

NOT FOUND AT GRAVEYARDS.

From time immemorial ghosts and graveyards have been an alliterative combination. No ghosts infest Hollywood, or Oakwood, or the ancient sepulchers of St. John's burying ground.

"I have been here nigh on eight year," said Keeper Simmons, of the Confederate section of Hollywood, in an interview with a Times man, "and nary a ghost has I seen. They has better manners than to fool around soldiers graves," he continued, and then he launched into a war narrative of such thrilling detail that a spook, hearing it, would have been frightened out of its few filmy garments or called for its smelling bottles.

NOT THE GENUINE ARTICLE.

In the old section of Hollywood fifteen or twenty years ago great excitement was occasioned, not only in the neighborhood, but throughout the city, by the appearance of an uncanny figure. For three days a white-clothed form acting queerly in the old section kept up the popular excitement, until finally, it was discovered that the supposed ghost was a crazy woman who had taken up her abode among the tombs.

Forty or fifty year ago two pirates were hanged in what is known as Penitentiary Bottom. The signal for the execution was a series of taps on a bell. The details of the execution were such as to excite a feeling of horror, the rope breaking with one of the condemned men who was hanged a second time. One of the penitentiary officers, who lived in Cary street, going from his home in the institution, had to pass the graves of the two men, who were buried near the scene of the execution. One night while in a hurry to reach the penitentiary, the officer on nearing the twin graves, had has his attention attracted by something white on the graves. A peculiar sensation was produced in the feelings of the officer, who hesitated to continue his journey. Finally, however, he decided to go ahead, but was seized with the greatest terror when the clear notes of a bell sounded in the still night. He turned to beat a precipitate retreat, when a white calf with a bell about its neck arose from between the graves and gave a reassuring bleat.

WHERE GHOSTS MIGHT APPEAR.

Has the reader ever visited Hollywood or Oakwood after dark? Assuredly, he would be awed, if not frightened, in approaching the dense midnight expanse of trees and shrubbery, whose silent, black depths are not relieved by a solitary gleam of light anywhere. Even the white of the marble tombstones vanishes with night. The contrast when a storm brewing and fitful flashes of lightening illumine the earth, is almost startling. On such a night the dwellers on adjacent streets bounding the cities of the dead might well be believed in the recital of some weird sight conjured up by a credulous mind in which the imaginative facility had been abnormally developed. Yet not one of these has ever seen a graveyard ghost, and gave a most matter-of-fact cold, negative reply when questioned by a reporter as to their experiences while living in what is popularly, but is erroneously, called a ghost neighborhood.

NOT SUPERSTITIOUS

Two colored laborers were encountered yesterday in Oakwood. They laughed when asked if they knew a good ghost story and expressed very positive disbelief in the supernatural. The reporter's heart was made sad when they said that "Uncle Jim," an aged darkey was a fund of ghost tales, whose habitat is in or near the cemetery, was down town and probably enjoying his accustomed Saturday social session. Could Uncle Jim have been tackled while in a bibulous and, therefore, communicative humor, a harvest of supernatural experiences would assuredly have been granted.

CITY HALL "HAUNTED."

City Hall is open to suspicion of being haunted. It stands on the site formerly occupied by the First Presbyterian church, old City Hall, State Chemist Taylor's laboratory and office and other structures. Among the colored population Dr. Taylor's place was looked upon with exceeding great suspicion by reason of its being the depository from time to time of various and sundry human remains. The evil associations of the old building, according to authorities on ghosts, cling to the present City Hall. So far as can be learned, however, the building is "haunted" only by persistent office seekers, some of whom do not stand even the "ghost" of a chance of ever becoming "familiar spirits" about the place.

The Virginian-Pilot, Norfolk, Virginia, September 8, 1899, pg. 5.

A REAL "SPOOK."
A Colored Man's Experience With A Norfolk County Ghost.

There is a story going the rounds of Norfolk county to the effect that a "ghost," and a real ghost, with all its ghastly raiments, exists in a vacant cabin near the city, but a certain old colored man in the county fell heir to a small fortune a few days ago and concluded to purchase the land on which this cabin is located. Hearing rumors, however, that a "ghost" really existed there, he concluded to go out and spend one night to see how the "land lay." He did not really believe in "spooks" or "ghosts," but as he was about to invest his money there he wanted certain. He is more than certain of it now. After he had gone out to the place and locked it securely from the outside, he took a seat on a log in front of the cabin to await developments. He did not have to wait. "Mr. Ghost" stepped quietly up behind him and tapping him lightly on the shoulder announced in a deep voice: "My friend, there is but two of left." It took the old fellow a good while to summon to his aid courage enough to answer: "Yas, sah, and if yo' gibs me a minit's start dar won't be but one left."

He broke all previous horse records down the road for seven or eight solid miles without even stopping or looking back to view the rear. Finally he did so, and, seeing nothing in sight, dropped heavily on a tree stump by the road to catch his breath. He only caught one good one, as "Mr. Ghost" suddenly loomed up and said in a harsh voice: "My friend, we have had a pretty hot race." "Yas," said the darkey, "and with your kind permission we am gwine to hab anoder [another] one right now." The race was resumed and ended only when the darkey fell exhausted by the roadside. The "ghost" disappeared and nothing has been seen of it since.

It is safe to add, however, that a real estate dealer cannot get a "pleasant look" from this darkey, as he is not in the land-buying business.

The Staunton Spectator and Vindicator, Staunton, Virginia, September 29, 1899, pg. 1.

DEAD ON THE RAIL
And Discovered by a Conductor in a Peculiar Manner.
WAS WARNED BY A GHOST
While Asleep in the Caboose—A Railroad Man's Story of an
Incident Which Occurred on the Norfolk and Western.

"One occurrence that may be substantiated by the records of the Norfolk & Western railway leads me to believe that the dead sometimes come back to earth," said A. M. Strong, an old railroad man, in conversation with a Chicago Inter-Ocean reporter. "A year and a half has elapsed since the occurrence, but despite the efforts of the family and friends of the dead man, assisted by one of the most powerful organizations of railroad men in the country, it still remains a mystery that will forever remain behind the gray curtains of death.

"A year ago last March I was in Roanoke, Va., on my way back West. I had hustled all day to get out, but at 9 o'clock that night I was still on the 'waiting list.' It was Sunday, and few freight trains were running. My 'card' was not good on passenger trains. Pay fare I could not, and so I was obliged to await the courtesy of some fellow O. R. C. (Order of Railway Conductors) man for transportation. There was to be a run west at 10 o'clock, and the yardmaster had agreed to 'square' me with the conductor. When he showed up I was introduced to him, and my card made me all right for a ride. His name is R. L. Ryan, and he is a typical railroad man in every way. Big and hearty, well educated and with the nerve so necessary in a vocation so hazardous, he is just the man for the business. The night was pleasant, and for a hour or two I sat in the cupola of the caboose talking with Ryan. It was nearing midnight when I went below and arranged a place to lie down.

"I had been asleep some time when I was awakened by the howling wind and the dashing rain on the metal roof of the caboose. The train was standing on a side track at Curve Siding, a little station away up in the Blue Ridge mountains, and an awful storm was in progress. I sat up and looked around the car. On the seat opposite me sat the engineer; he had come back to the caboose and was looking over some orders, while Ryan still occupied the seat in the cupola, but now asleep, with his head resting against the glass of the window at his side. As I watched him he opened his eyes, and, looking down at me, asked:

"Who was that fellow who was here just now? Where did he go?"

"I told him no one had been in the car except the engineer and the negro brakeman, who was dozing in a corner at the rear of the car. Baldwin, the engineer, said: 'Bob, you've been dreaming. If you want to sleep, why don't you lie down like a white man.'

"'I want to watch for No. 4,' Ryan replied. 'Maybe I was asleep, I hope so, had a mighty nasty dream.'

"He leaned back against the window and was soon snoring again. I went to the door of the caboose and looked out. The rain was falling in torrents, and it was the darkest night I ever saw. The only visible object was the window of the depot, through which gleamed dimly the light on the table of the night telegraph operator. I started back from the door to my seat, when Ryan jumped down the cupola, almost striking me in his haste, picked up his lantern from the floor, and started for the door, saying:

"'God! That's twice I've seen that man, and he's told me both times to go and pick up that body at the end of the platform.'

"His face was white and drawn, and he was trembling like a leaf. The negro brakeman cowered back in his corner and his eyes showed only the white as he said: 'Cap'n Bob's done got a spell.'

"Ryan, bareheaded and with no coat on, dashed out in the drenching rain. We could see his lantern dancing as he went running up the track until finally it disappeared behind the broad cotton platform that stood between the main line and the siding. Just as his lantern passed out of sight, we heard the low hoarse roar of a duplex whistle. It was the 'Virginia Limited,' No. 4, giving the station signal, less than a mile away. When the sound of the whistle died away, he heard Ryan calling:

"'Hi! Baldwin! Send that nigger, over here to help me move this body.'

"The colored man turned a shade lighter; his eyes rolled up, and in a piteous tone he said: 'Gawd, Mistah John, I ain't gwine to touch no dead corpses dis night. Ah'll quit foh Ah does.'

"'Hurry up, John,' came Rayan's voice. 'No. 4's coming.'

"Through the pouring rain the engineer and myself went up the track to where Ryan was standing. By the dim light of the lantern we saw lying on the track, the horribly mangled corpse of a white man. We rolled the poor, mutilated remains in a blanket and as soon as No. 4 passed carried it to the depot. Then Ryan and the now thoroughly terrified darky searched the track in both directions for something that would identify the remains. Plenty of evidence was found in the torn clothing that was strewn along the track in both directions from the spot, where the body was found. He had evidently met his fate early in the night, for the body had been dragged back and forth along the track for nearly a quarter of a mile.

"At least a hundred yards from where Ryan made his grewsome discovery he found a part of a torn and bloody vest and in the inside pocket were a traveling card of the O. R. C. (Order of Railway Conductors), issued to Harvey W. Sharmell of Division, Ohio, an insurance policy, and a small sum of money. There were also two or three letters from friends in Bradford Junction, O. This was all.

"Whether he had been on one of the passenger trains and had been robbed and thrown off, or had been riding on a freight and had fallen between the cars, the best efforts of the railroad police failed to determine. The body was taken charge of by the O. R. C. and was sent to his home in Ohio for burial.

"Again, I ask the question: Do the dead ever come back? If not, what was the influence that prompted Ryan to go so surely to the very spot where that body lay? Was it the disembodied spirit of the dead man unwilling to see its earthly tenement still further mangled? Who can tell?

"R. L. Ryan is still a conductor on the Norfolk and Western railway, and lived at No. 357 Salem avenue, Roanoke, Va., and John Baldwin is now round-house foreman for some railroad at Lynchburg, Va. Both are men of truth and integrity, and neither of them is in the least superstitious."

About the Author

Michelle L. Hamilton earned her MA in history from San Diego State University. Hamilton is the author or editor of several books including *"I Would Still Be Drowned in Tears": Spiritualism in Abraham Lincoln's White House* and *Mary Ball Washington: The Mother of George Washington*. She has published articles in *The Morbid Curious* and *The Feminine Macabre*. Her latest books *Civil War Ghosts* and *Haunted Land* are published by Haunted Road Media. A lifelong student of history, Hamilton has worked as a docent at several museums across the county. She is currently the manager of the Mary Washington House in Fredericksburg, VA.

You can follow her at her blog Paranormal History at https://paranormalhist.blogspot.com.

Other Haunted Road Media titles from Michelle L. Hamilton:

The 18th Century is one of the most fascinating and complex eras in history. It was an era of enlightenment and revolution. New innovations in science and manufacturing improved the lives of millions. A band of committed patriots in the American colonies sparked a revolution that defeated the world's largest empire. It was an era that helped usher in the modern world.

But it was also an era were the belief in witches, ghosts, and sorcery was prevalent. The belief in supernatural forces stood in contrast with enlightenment thinking, which embraced a more rational view of the world backed by scientific study and experimentation. This conflict between old world thinking and the enlightenment played out in the popular press of the 18th Century in both England and its American colonies.

HAUNTED LAND uncovers the paranormal tales of Colonial America as told through the newspapers of the time...

For more information visit:
www.hauntedroadmedia.com

www.ingramcontent.com/pod-product-compliance
Lightning Source LLC
Chambersburg PA
CBHW020243130626
46549CB00005B/2039